AN INSIDER'S GUIDE

TO

BUYING OR SELLING

A HOME

By Kevin Sime

Disclaimer

This book is a simplified guide to buying and/or selling a home and is not meant to be a substitute for legal advice.

Please contact an attorney before you enter into any real estate contract or transaction.

No portion of this book may be copied or reproduced without the expressed permission from the author.

TABLE OF CONTENTS

Dedication

This book is dedicated as a thank you to those who have helped and taught me along this journey: especially Victoria, Mom (executive vice president of marketing) and Ed, Dad, Genie and Alex, Go Go and Hank, Adele and Eddie, David and Ann Marie, Sean and Sarah, Genna and Henry, Brendan & Liam, Peter, Carol, John and Katie Sime, Jim Sime, Algene Elliot & Charlotte McCord, Scott McCord & Tracy Dugan, Billy Mandel, Kenny Mandel, Jaime Silver, Jay, Joanie, Jordan & Jill Slutsky, Lorie Slutsky & Mercedes Leon, Mitchell, Syndee, Amanda & Perri Slutsky, Eric and Liz Sher, Steve Eichner, Carrie Blakeman, Kristin Stills, Brian Daniels, Cliff Ament, Edward Mozzar, Anthony Marotta, Larry Guli, Craig Mele, Mario Taglic, Peter Kuperschmid, Joseph Veroba, Marty Itzkowitz, MJ Goff, Adam Butter, Leah Tozer, Sonia Dale, Barbara Ruotolo, Carmela Urso, and Susan Paraspolo, Matt Miller, Johnny Barnes and Safe Harbor Inspections.

Special thanks to my dream team…Heather Miles, Christie Miles, Aunt Linda Hornick.

And, to every client in my construction and my real estate career, thank you for all you've taught me.

A Note From The Author:

My intentions behind this guide and my promise to you---

Buying or selling your home is one of life's biggest and most stressful events as well as one of the most exciting and life changing. As one of the largest purchases you'll ever make, it's loaded with tiny details and unexpected issues regardless of whether selling on your own or working with an experienced real estate agent.

If you've not been involved in a real estate transaction in a number of years, a lot has changed in the process. My goal is to put some of these changes down on paper. I also want to provide a more in-depth understanding of the process so readers will avoid costly mistakes. My promise to you is that once you've read these pages, you'll be a much more informed customer whether or not you choose to use my services.

My choice to become a real estate agent evolved after owning my remodeling business. As the business grew, I formed very successful relationships with my clients. As these relationships flourished, my clients began asking for my assistance with buying or selling their homes. I enjoy this work very much and so my hope is to educate first time buyers/sellers as well as the existing homeowner who is ready to downsize or upsize.

I hope you will take advantage of the information here; take this book with you when looking at properties or use it as a guide when it's time to get your home ready for sale.

-   Kevin Sime

"Real Estate cannot be lost or stolen, nor can it be carried away. Purchased with common sense, paid in full and managed with reasonable care, it is about the safest investment in the world."

Franklin D. Roosevelt

PART 1: SELLING YOUR HOME

CHAPTER 1

Compare, Compare, Compare

One of the biggest mistakes that sellers make is putting their property on the market without a true understanding of what the property is worth. Just because your neighbor's 3-bedroom, 2-bath ranch sold for $500,000 does not mean that yours will sell in that same price range. While you may think, "It's on the same block, it's in the same shape and has the same number of rooms" that misjudgment will most likely cost you thousands or may extend the amount of time that you have your house on the market, hurting your sale in the end.

For example, let's call your neighbor Joe… Joe's home features an updated kitchen with stainless steel appliances, high hats, a center kitchen island with sink, cherry wood cabinets and quartz countertops. In comparison your own kitchen may not have been updated for ten years, you may have older appliances, your cabinets look inexpensive/shabby and you have an old-fashioned chandelier-type lamp fixture centered over your kitchen table. Many say the kitchen is the heart of the house and it's where the family meets more than any other space. Buyers today consider the kitchen the most important room in the house and a noteworthy fact is that they don't want to update it right away paying another $10,000+ to do so. Buyers ideally want all the upscale amenities.

For those of you "for sale by owners" out there, you need to do your research to determine how your home compares to those that have sold in your neighborhood. The two obvious dangers are under pricing your home where you lose $10-$30,000 if not more or overpricing your home and having it sit on the market longer than it should. The length a listing stays on the market starts speculation that there may something terribly wrong with the home. It also involves the added time and expense of additional carrying costs as well as the energy to keep your home ready to show on a daily basis.

The fact is the home is a great buy but just priced too high in comparison with other local listings. One outcome of this is the need to underprice the home in order to get buyers through the door. In later chapters, I will discuss: staging a home, marketing the home and negotiating the deal. The takeaway from this section is to consider having your home professionally appraised or invite two or three reputable real estate agents to come in to provide an honest opinion based on their professional research. Doing this may mean taking a little extra time to get your house ready to list on the market. My experience shows it is a wise move to achieve your desired outcome.

CHAPTER 2

Understanding the Home-Selling Process

Let's face it...you've lived in your home for decades, raised your kids there and the home itself is now an honorary family member! You know just where the floor squeaks, that ticking sound that the furnace makes, and you have grown accustomed to that slight shift in the staircase that leads to the bedrooms. However, once you know you are ready to sell your home, you have to start distancing yourself from this attachment. Remember at its core, the house is simply wood, nails, a roof and walls. To state it plainly, your home is an investment to the buyer and they want the best investment they can make. If you let your emotions take over, your judgment as a seller will be clouded with misguided reasoning. You may mistakenly turn away some very good offers that come your way. You might even convince yourself that the price the appraiser/real estate agent advises to be the market value of your home is incorrect. It's safe to say that just because you have the measurements of the heights of your kids on the kitchen wall doesn't mean your home is worth $20,000 more. Your memories are just that: *YOUR* MEMORIES. The buyer wants to make NEW MEMORIES in the home they will cherish. A local town I know of received the "Tree City Award" a few years ago from an environmental group. Sure, the town has a lot of trees and the town has also been on the list of "more desirable places to live" but do these accolades add value? Does the home deserve to be sold for $20,000 more than a similar home a few blocks away? The answer is almost always no. Accolades that your town has received in the past were great for that time but have little or no bearing on pricing a home today. What matters more is the condition of the house itself: are aspects of your home outdated, in need of repair and/or a fresh coat of paint, has your roof seen better days? As a seller, your mission is to find a buyer who is excited about your home and is willing to pay the highest price. In order to do that, your home has to shine brighter in relation to the other comparable properties that are for sale locally. The first impression of the home must be memorable and should allow the buyer to be able to see themselves living in it. To that end, I suggest the seller create, utilize and review a "to-do" list so when those buyers pull up to the curb, they are instantly wowed and can't wait to put in an offer. At times I have even advised clients to send their landscaper over to the neighbor's house (with permission, of course) to make the surrounding properties look even more appealing.

The philosophy behind setting the listing price

There are a variety of factors when pricing a home. The neighborhood the home is located in is one of them. Is the school district a desirable one?   How unique is the home? What is the home's physical condition?   Can the seller sit on the listing or do they need to move it quickly? The answers to these questions as well as others provide what is often called the "pricing strategy" and something I have significant experience in. The pricing strategy has an art to it with a proven established formula of success. What does this mean for the seller? Frankly, the seller needs to be willing to set aside their own beliefs about the monetary value of their home. Sometimes what a realtor will suggest is not the price you thought or hoped but you should hear them out as to why. The experience can be an eye-opening one. The best realtor for you can give you several reasons for the price they are suggesting. Many sellers wind up trying to sell their home based upon what they think the house should list for and this is usually a big mistake.

Recent statistics show that more than 80% of all FSBO's wind up listing and selling with a realtor. Statistics also show that FSBO's also sell for considerably less than homes sold by a qualified Realtor. Trying the FSBO route will most likely take away profits from your bottom line. The process of carrying costs, taxes, etc., and time spent holding onto the home as you attempt to sell yourself is something you should certainly factor into your budget. Not to mention the strain of having to live in a home that is always ready to show. Having your life on hold is not enjoyable and isn't practical either.

Ultimately, a realtor averages a higher sales price value over FBSO's as negotiations are often more difficult without a realtor's experienced involvement. Beware of the agent that will list your home at your higher assumed price based on your false market assumptions. You will most likely sign a 6 to 12 month contract and be tied to an agent that doesn't have your best interests at heart

There are three terms realtors use when coming up with the price of a house: *market value, appraisal value*, and *assessed value*. Here is a brief explanation of each:

Market Value is what the house can sell for and in order to determine this an experienced realtor compares other similar properties that have sold in a one-mile radius and preferably within the last 6 months. Simply it is what the market has established as the selling price based upon similar homes in the neighborhood.

Appraisal value is the price that is set by a certified appraiser either ordered by the bank, mortgage or insurance company. There are private appraisal companies that operate on their own and can provide an appraisal value for a seller before their home goes on the market. If you are using me as your realtor, I can discuss with you the positives and negatives regarding choosing this route to determine your home's appraised value. Just yesterday, I had a property in contract for 950k. The Mortgage company sent their appraiser to do their due diligence. The home appraised at 915k and the buyer would not have gotten their mortgage and as such were preparing to back out of the deal. The sellers reduced the sale price to 915k and we were able to continue moving the deal ahead.

Assessed value is what municipalities use when determining the amount of property tax to impose. The values of all three many not always corroborate with each other, as each one uses a different set of criteria.

An interesting fact to note is that a large portion of homes are assessed higher than their market value but that, unfortunately, is how the system works. Speaking of assessed value, let's say your new home was purchased at 500k but it assesses at 600k. March right into the tax assessor's office and request a tax reduction immediately on the property taxes!

Do you know what your home is worth?

The internet is very useful and the first research tool that a potential seller should investigate when hoping to find out the value of their home. There are a lot of online tools that can assist in providing an estimate. Be wary of just filling out the fields providing information to random websites though as they may be scammers recording, compiling and possibly using your information. Websites I consult are: MLSLI, Zillow, and Realtor.com. Also, I have my own APP which is user friendly and I will gladly send it to you just ask! These sites I've mentioned here have recorded prices of recent home sales.

Their figures are based on your home's age, zip code and amenities: number of bedrooms, baths, interior square footage, etc. These websites have a quick pricing formula that can provide an estimate in seconds. Be warned these sites should only be used as a guide because since this is a free tool, you cannot be sure how updated/accurate their records are. A good suggestion is to visit a few and see how they average out. Make no mistake, there is no way for a computer to accurately price a home. It is a guestimate using averages and algorithms. I am frequently asked to price a property either on the phone or on the spot. I price my properties doing hard research and comps after seeing the condition of the home inside and out in person.

One of the most accurate, if not the MOST accurate way of determining your home's value is by calling in a professional appraiser. They will provide the best "market value" amount by using up to date tools like comparative sales, considering the interior square footage, the condition and age of the property, size, proximity to schools, parks and commuting routes. When appraising they also take into consideration when updates were made to crucial areas in the home such as the roof, furnace, hot water heater, appliance replacement as well as other factors.

The appraiser will provide an unbiased market value since they have no interest in the outcome. Their figures are used for a variety of reasons such as: to assist a lender in determining the amount of a loan, or a seller to determine what they should sell the property for or a buyer to ascertain if they are getting their money's worth for their investment.

The services of any appraiser while invaluable are not free, and a quality appraisal may cost around $500.00. Ultimately, in my professional opinion, it is a small price to pay to potentially make you thousands more in a sale or cost you thousands by not selling your "over-priced For Sale by Owner" home. I also know several appraisers who I've worked with and trust and will gladly provide their contact information upon request.

Lastly, a real estate professional will be able to provide insight and a wealth of information on how the homes have been selling in your neighborhood. Experienced realtors have tools and formulas for determining market value. Ultimately, the market value is based on the price that a buyer and seller agree upon together. Experience builds knowledge and logically who would most often have this information handy other than a real estate agent? A real estate agent can provide you a CMA or a "Comparative Market Analysis" which is a selection of homes that are relatively identical to yours, within a close distance, and what they sold for during the past 6 months. A notable fact is that since market fluctuations are based on the time of year, mortgage rates and other contributing factors, 6 months has been determined to be the best time frame to use in a CMA. Real estate agents do not charge for a CMA when they visit with prospective sellers.

A CMA is used as a way for the agent to sell their services to the buyer, and to let the buyer know their reasons for suggesting this or that price. Those looking to put their house on the market should consult with 2 or more agents before they choose which one to work with, so they get a feel as to which agent has the experience and understanding to price the house right. When an agent comes to your home for a CMA meeting, use this time to ask all your questions. Each time you speak with an agent is a learning opportunity.

While I have discussed many aspects that affect the price of a home: age, condition, amenities, style, etc., there are still more variables that are a bit more difficult to uncover. How a municipality determines a home's "assessed value" in order to apply the property taxes is a good example of this. Other contributing factors could be whether circumstances/changes are coming to the community, such as a new industrial park or a new local condominium. Once the listing price is determined there is no guarantee that buyers will come running with offers. So much has to be taken care of to prepare for the potential buyer to see that your house is worth the asking price...or even possibly more! A home can be divided into three parts: the actual dwelling itself: the floor, walls, roof, ceilings, etc. This part is the home's "skeleton" so to speak. Then there is the second part which is the design of the house: overall aesthetic, paint colors, color of fixtures, layout etc. The third is the mechanicals, the boiler and hot water heater, electrical service, HVAC, sprinklers, as well as the condition of appliances which are oftentimes over looked by the buyer and seller but mark my words, they are never overlooked by a home inspector and will usually hamper a smooth transaction.

All these design and mechanical features and or issues can affect whether the house sits on the market for longer than need be or if the seller gets their asking price quickly and with little grief. Selling your home should be a partnership between an expert in the field who will determine the market value. After that, the seller needs to do all they can to make the home desirable and attractive to potential buyers. When they come in the buyer should be able to visualize themselves and their family living in the home you are selling. Neutral paint colors, removing excessive artwork and family photos are simple yet low cost fixes.

"Universalizing" your home means to this realtor that you are giving it mass appeal by taking away the many personal touches such as photographs and adding design touches like accent pillows or drapes that enhance the home to the buyer's eye. Can the buyers see themselves living in this home?   That is the kind of interior you most certainly want to create.

A lot of time and effort is needed from both the seller and their agent to get the best price for your home and to sell it quickly. Homes that tend to linger on the market start getting a whispered reputation or speculation that there is something seriously wrong when often the only issue is that the asking price was too high. The same is true when a home's price keeps going down which also portrays a negative impression. I know some sellers who were caught in a similar trap and ended up taking their house off of the market for a few months and then putting it back on the market at a more realistic price and it sold quickly. They just needed to price it right.

CHAPTER 3

Should You Sell It On Your Own? The FSBO Dilemma

For Sale By Owner/Amateur Selling is all the rage now between Facebook Marketplace, eBay, Amazon, Craigslist, Let go etc. Most people believe that they can sell anything themselves online. You might have success getting rid of your kid's toys they outgrew, used electronics and cars but a house is one of the most expensive and valuable investments you have made in your life. The one thing that you have taken care of and maintained for years. To just sell it for less than it's worth seems like a complete shame. The mistake many folks make is they think that a transaction such as this is an easy-peasy endeavor. I hate to burst your bubble; it isn't easy, and it is a process not to be taken lightly. I want to explain some of the reasons why.

The term FSBO (pronounced fizz-bow) pretty much means what it says: selling your home on your own without any outside help from a realtor, foregoing a consultation and/or appraisal. The thought is that the seller will walk away with top price and save the deducted 4-6% standard commission his or her agent would receive. There is something to be said about "doing it yourself" but not in the case of the sale of such a prized possession. Even when it comes to the final stages of the closing, the seller should always have a qualified real estate attorney review the contract. While you may think that selling your house on your own may be worth it, considering the popularity of internet sites devoted to the subject, the fact is that only a very small percentage of homes (approximately 8%) are sold through a FSBO sale. Why? Well, here's the scoop on that:

What is your time worth?

In my years of experience with handling real estate transactions I have come to the conclusion and opinion that many folks who call themselves "buyers" are not, they are really just curious. Some "buyers" are just testing the waters and seeing what's out there. Sometimes one partner wants to buy something, but the other partner is coming along reluctantly. While I know that taking them out to see houses is pretty much a waste of time, I still do it. Why you ask? Well, it's my job and my clients may not buy now but I am always hopeful they will remember me when they are more serious and ready.

Imagine as an FSBO'er waiting around to show your home. Excitedly you schedule five showings in a weekend. You spruce up the interior, put away the clutter, toys and dishes. Maybe you even spice up the air with a nice cinnamon candle and then you watch as five couples walk in and walk out. They may say they'll "be in touch" or just a plain "thank you" or nothing at all as they leave. (Those of us in the business call them "looky-loos.") The real question is: did these showings take hours of your time to complete? Was it worth it to kick your family out of the house, awaken your child from a nap to relocate them or delay a social event? I hope you get where I am headed with this. Truth is that you as an FSBO'er may end up doing this for weeks...or maybe months and it will be a strain. Are you up for that?

On average, a home may need to be shown thirty times if not more! There may be a lot of properties in the area giving buyers a large inventory to view. For example, you've just gotten home from a busy day at work. You get a phone call that a potential buyer is in the neighborhood and would like to see your home. What do you do? Will you scramble for this last-minute showing? Race around with a mop and the Dust buster? Lock your pet in the crate? Simply to appease the casual buyer who has no intention of buying your home. Seemingly you will. As time passes this repeated preparation process will become very frustrating as well as exasperating and to what end? I do my job because your time, your peace and your family are more valuable than that.

Having an experienced real estate agent as part of your home-selling process is like having prices on every item at a garage sale: preparation, no mysteries, the information you need at your fingertips and little or no awkwardness as it applies to such an important transaction. That is my job and I did not become experienced at it overnight.

How much do you REALLY know about selling a home?

If you have never personally done a real estate transaction, imagine the stress that arrives with an offer to buy your home. If you are one of those 8% who get a bite on their sale do you know the next steps? Are you confident you priced it right? A quick offer or multiple bids may suggest you have priced it too low. How would you handle multiple bids? I cannot help but feel that taking on an FSBO is like someone acting as their own defense attorney in a murder case.

Real estate agents, real estate attorneys and appraisers spend a lot of time learning the business and the jungle of legal requirements. With their experience these people can provide remedies if and when problems arise and are an extra layer of security. Recently, I had a seller find out right before closing that their back yard deck did not have the proper town signoffs and permits. The deck had an old permit, so apparently their new deck was larger and not inspected by the building department of the municipality. The closing had to be postponed so the deck could be legalized otherwise the buyers would not be able to get a mortgage on a house that was not clearing title due to this oversight!

Luckily, in my line of work, I get to work with many professionals in all sorts of fields that may be helpful when complications such as this appear. A colleague of mine is an expeditor by trade. He is someone who is talented and knowledgeable about moving along an application for a permit. With his assistance, we rescheduled the closing and cleared the faulty permit issue for the deck. After that speed bump the closing went smoothly. If the same scenario happened for a FSBO transaction, the outcome may not have been the same.

Is your home ready to sell?

A good topic to discuss is preparing your home to sell. Will you know what to repair, what to replace and what to leave as is? A seasoned real estate agent's perspective is invaluable. They will come in and know immediately if the walls need to be repaired or repainted. Do the carpets need to be replaced or simply steam cleaned? Does the roof need to be replaced or should a few shingles be repaired? It is a daunting endeavor to walk around a house, crawl into the crawlspace and get up on the roof to assess each area. An agent will save you time, trouble, and a lot of grief by letting you know what to fix, and what you can possibly ignore. There is a line to draw in the sand when it comes to spending money in order to sell a home. Some projects will never pay a dividend and should be left alone.

How do you advertise your FSBO?

With all of the avenues available to market your FSBO, you may be feeling a bit overwhelmed. Should you advertise in the paper? Put up a yard sign? Create an ad on Facebook or Craigslist? Simply place it on Zillow, Trulia or the FSBO sites? What about all of the above? If you do create this ad what will you say about the house? Can you take attractive photos? Will you plan to schedule your own open house? A realtor has access to advanced systems to help you plan all of this.

One word of caution is worth mentioning. By putting your house on all of these free sites, there is a slight possibility that you may be putting yourself, your family and your valuables in jeopardy. The reality nowadays is that there are some scammers out there. They masquerade as a buyer to obtain access to your home. They may come with another person to distract you as they wander the house looking to steal something or to strategically "case" the home for a future burglary! A real estate agent's worthwhile role is to act as your screener. They should make sure that anyone they bring to your home is a qualified and serious buyer who is pre-approved for a mortgage.

One of the most important tools for buying and selling houses is the MLS aka The Multiple Listing Service. This is a very reputable, elaborate and detailed list of homes for sale. The agent working for an MLS seller will usually have professional photos taken, will create an enticing description of the home, (always accentuating the positives). This will interest other agents and buyers who also use MLS. There is no cost to a buyer utilizing MLS. In my local area, there are approximately 80,000 agents using the MLS system.

By listing with an agent on MLS, you have access to all those professionals who are working with buyers. Although you should be reminded that the MLS is not a magic pill. Even with that wealth of access to inventory and home-seekers it will still take time to sell your house. On average it takes a home six months to sell. Imagine how long it could take if you don't use MLS?

So, let's just say for the FSBO listing you've found a buyer and negotiated a sale price. What comes next? Do you know the paperwork involved to make this deal legal? Do you know the fair housing laws? There are legal disclosures to attend to, inspections, title search, bank appraisals and the like. Who will draw up the contract? Hopefully a real estate specific attorney. What will you do if the buyers come back with demands in the contract terms like reducing the price because of an aged roof, or asking that the electrical service be upgraded, etc.?

These sticking points can postpone the closing and cost the seller time/money with every delay. If these negotiations and preparations do not run smoothly you could easily lose the buyer if it appears the deal is not moving along at a constructive pace.

The art of the negotiation

You have your house on the market for $450,000 and you get an offer of $399,000. In this transaction did you price your home correctly? If you didn't price it correctly that $399,000 offer may be a winner. Alternatively, your stubborn hopes to get the price you have in mind may cloud your judgment and let a fair offer/counteroffer negotiation get away from you, thus collapsing the sale. Many deals have fallen through as FSBO sellers let their inexperience get in the way of the deal.

After all we've talked about up until now if you're still considering orchestrating an FSBO, I hope you will give it some hard thought and reconsider. All I want at the heart of this is for you to get started off on the right foot.

CHAPTER 4

Take My Advice...Please

My intent with this guide is to help you towards the most successful buying or selling experience. I've seen too many deals go sour because of simple missed steps or because a seller thought they could do it all on their own. Many sellers have gotten stuck and lost their buyer and their deal. Let me help you prevent that outcome.

Not doing your homework when pricing your home

It may seem like a good plan to base the price of your home on what your neighbor's house went for but it isn't. While your neighbor's house may be similar with the same number of bedrooms and square footage the similarities may halt right there. Only a realtor's tool of Comparative Market Analysis or a certified appraisal will provide the best formula for determining your home's asking price.

Choosing a realtor for all the wrong reasons

If you decide to go with a real estate agent, don't base your decision solely on the agent who says they can get you the highest price. What is promised and what is realistic can be two different things. If the agent can prove through their Comparative Market Analysis that they can get you top dollar that is a more credible route. You may want to ask that realtor for references from the last three customers they sold a property for. See the price the agent suggested and what it eventually sold for.   You'll be glad you did. I also suggest interviewing three or four agents and see how they answer your questions you have prepared for them. Do you feel comfortable with them?   Do they have a good record of sales?   Do they have a marketing plan for your home that makes sense to you?

Subjective Pricing

This happens a lot...a seller comes to me and tells me about the memories he and his family have had in their home over the years. He gives an account of the birthday parties, family reunions and the holidays spent there. The owner can't see putting the house on the market for the price I suggest. "But the mural my wife painted," he says.   What about our carefully manicured backyard? That has to account for something! It's a difficult conversation to have with the seller but the next owner does not care about paintings or how you tended to your backyard.

A buyer will be looking at your property with thoughts of making it their own. This is the key to success and the vibe you want in your house. I am talking about the feeling that every potential buyer that visits should be able visualize themselves in the home you are selling. Don't cloud pricing strategy with emotional attachment. Don't be tempted to muddle up pricing strategy by focusing too much on what you think you "need" to get financially. The whole concept of wanting to walk away with a profit is not very realistic all the time. "I need to get $1,000,000.00 for this home because I owe $850,000 and I need to be able to move on and buy something small to live in." Unfortunately, the market doesn't care what you owe or what you feel you need. Don't cloud the pricing strategy with your emotional or financial attachment to the home.

The first two weeks your house is on the market are key!

When a new home goes on the MLS system, it is announced to all the agents who have buyers for that neighborhood. Just as your agent knows what your house should be listed for, similarly, so do the other agents. They will look at other "comps", houses sold within your neighborhood and determine if your home is overpriced. Based on their research they might not even suggest your home to their clients. The reason being that the buyer's agent is looking for homes in their client's price range and to bring them to your home is a waste of time for everyone involved. If your home is priced correctly you will have a parade of agents coming and going. Perhaps even that popularity can spark a bidding war that may eventually get you more money than you originally planned.

A month passes by without any bites on the home and you agree to lower the price. At this point you may have lost some qualified buyers who were looking a month ago. Not to mention, potential new buyers will be wondering why the home's price was lowered. Buyer psychology could suggest something was discovered to be very wrong with the property. This scenario is totally preventable by pricing the house correctly, using good local knowledge and an accurate comparative marketing analysis. For those of you not in a hurry, testing the waters may be a bad idea. Some sellers like to list their home for a higher price just to see what will happen.

As mentioned above, that game can hurt the sale down the road if you decide to reduce the price. Maybe you're thinking that the market is going to improve, and you will find sellers ready to make a desirable offer. My suggestion is to put the house up for sale when you're fully ready and to list it at the appropriate price. Why put yourself through the torture of gambling with your most valuable asset? Playing Russian roulette with the housing market is another tactic to avoid.

Say your home went on the market at a high price with the idea that you'll just drop it in three months. Then, the housing market in your neighborhood drops dramatically for a reason such as sudden increase in inventory. Now as a result, you can get burned and you have to drop your house price significantly more than you originally thought. One word of advice is once you've put your house on the market; keep your eye on housing prices to catch any negative trends in the works.

Have any repairs to make? Don't sit on getting an estimate

I've seen it happen where a seller knew that the roof was in need of repair but figured he would wait until he had an offer. Without getting his own estimate, he allowed the buyer to reduce the offer considerably more than a new roof would cost. If the seller had done the homework to get a few estimates, the final price of the house would have been in line with cost of the roof repair as well as the probability of a higher offer from the onset.

Keep the lights on

If you are not going to live in the house while it's on the market, keep the electricity and heat on so that water pipes do not freeze, and also so that when buyers tour the property, they are not seeing their breath in the air. Keep it at a comfortable temperature. I really enjoy showing a home in the heat of the summer and the buyers will not turn on an air conditioner. Not only does it show that the appliance works and the house is comfortable, it is smart to have a buyer linger and spend time seeing themselves living there. I have seen buyers not even view an entire home due to heating or cooling missteps from sellers. Nobody wants to be uncomfortable when they are shopping for a pair of jeans or buying a home!

Staging a home is worth every penny

You may not have given this any thought but staging a home by a professional designer can do wonders for a fast sale and getting your desired price. This stager can bring in temporary art pieces, antique furniture and may only cost a small percentage of the price you want to get for your home. All real estate agents should be able to suggest two or three stagers you can consult with. Another option is to rearrange your home with what you already have using a designer's eye to make it look current and appealing.

Let buyers see your home in the best light

We're all trying to downsize and declutter. Doing so seems to be all the rage now. The one place where this is crucial is when buyers are coming into the home for the first time. They will and should look in closets, basements, garages, crawl spaces and in every room. Keeping these areas chock full of stuff is going to turn off a potential buyer. You want to show a home not a storage locker.

"Buyers decide within the first eight seconds of seeing a home if they are interested in buying it, get out of your car, walk in their shoes and see what they see in the first eight seconds"

Barbara Corcoran

Take some time to review your home and make sure the little details are in order: screens in need of repair, stove tops that need a good cleaning and dusty windowsills. When you live in a house you tend to overlook areas like this but a fresh pair of eagle eyes will spot fixes like these and an experienced agent will do that for you. Have someone walk through your house to point out these "ISSUES" before you put it on the market. Better yet, have a real estate agent do a walk through and make a list of projects to do right away versus those that can wait.

Telling the truth and nothing but the whole truth

There are parts of a home that need to be in good working order such as: the roof, the hot water heater, the septic system, plumbing and electricity aka the big items. The seller needs to know the status of these important areas and these should be disclosed to potential buyers. If you are dishonest, a sale may be delayed or cancelled. Take responsibility for the condition of your home and be honest. Full disclosure is in your best interest and is the moral and legal thing to do. A seller who knows there are issues with their home and does not disclose them can be personally liable. If the roof is leaky, you need to either repair it or agree to a lower price to offset the repair the buyer will plan to do. The roof will come up at some point so be upfront about it.

Having an inspector come in to do a home evaluation makes sense so you can get a heads up on problems you didn't even know existed. It is best to know in advance rather than after you find a buyer and contracts begin to be prepared.

Are you qualified?

If your plan is to purchase another home after selling yours, you should get yourself qualified for your next mortgage. The home you are selling may only pay partially toward your new purchase and you want to be ready to step into that new home right after closing on the old one. Get in touch with your lender as soon as you put your home on the market to make sure you're in a good place for the next purchase.

Is your buyer able to buy?

One of the biggest reasons for working with a real estate agent is that they don't want to waste anyone's time: the seller's, the buyers or their own by showing any home to buyers who are not qualified. Most real estate agents will not even talk to a buyer unless they are qualified for a mortgage that will more than pay for a home in the neighborhood which they are looking in.

Keep in mind if the buyer needs advice on mortgage companies, an agent can certainly suggest several options to them. If you are selling without using an agent you need to ask any buyer who makes an offer if they are preapproved and get a copy of their commitment letter. Plain and simple there is no use spending time and energy for a buyer who is not able to borrow the money to buy your home.

Sticking around during the showing

When showings are scheduled make yourself scarce. Go out for coffee. Don't be waiting in the wings as you might spook a buyer and may not like what you hear. Buyers can be tough on a home and a seller may take it personally. There may also be those who are interested but feel uncomfortable with the owner around and do not want to offend anyone. The prospective buyer may not be able to think of themselves living in the home with the seller present or be afraid to ask questions. They may not want to discuss how they'd change a room around. The feeling of being watched may inhibit their excitement about buying your home. The solution is to let your agent answer any questions that are asked during a showing. Your agent is very experienced with how best to word answers. I am not being deceitful but there are things the potential buyer has to find out for themselves, like the quality of the school district, and crime statistics. There are also fair housing laws to consider as well as many others. Do you know what you are permitted to say to a buyer or a seller? I can guarantee an experienced agent is very familiar with the current laws because the fines can be serious!

The first offer may be the only one

I tell my clients this all the time. If you get an offer on the house which is close to asking, don't think that this may just be the beginning of a great bidding war. Odds are your house is not going to generate more money than you first thought. That scenario doesn't happen very often. My advice: if you want to sell, and you get a good offer, it may be the only offer. Don't be quick to turn it down or delay in responding.

It's okay to be friendly, but not too much

During a showing, you may feel very comfortable with the potential buyers. Doing so may mean dropping your guard. For instance, you may start getting too chatty and let things slip out that may affect the sale. Not only are your buyers there to see if they like the house but to also find things that turn them off about it. You may not want to talk about the noise from the jets that fly over the house or the traffic that comes down the street on Sunday. Don't give your buyers any tidbit that makes them cross your home off of their list.

Watch what is said in discussing items related to the house and neighborhood. Remember, this could be their new home. You're no doubt excited about moving on. But buyers will naturally start second-guessing. A casual statement about the house being too small for a growing family or the schools are going through some changes, might be enough innocent chatter to squash their interest.

I recently had a client refuse to fix anything that was needed to sell her home and then disclose a laundry list to her attorney before closing. The attorney had a legal responsibility to disclose the information to the buyer's attorney. What do you think happened?

The buyers demanded all the items be corrected and fixed before moving forward and I don't blame them at all. I warned my client that it would hold up the sale but she didn't care. It wound up hurting her in the long run because she lost a house she really loved due to the fact that her home couldn't sell quick enough.

The Closing Costs -- Do you really know what's involved?

The only amount of money in the buyer's head is how much they are paying for the house. Something to consider is that there is a whole list of items that need to be paid before the keys are handed over. For instance:

- The percentages of commissions paid to the real estate agent(s). Usually the seller's responsibility.
- Attorney and title agent fees. Buyers Responsibility.
- Excise/gains tax/ flip tax (if applicable). Responsibility varies.
- Money owed for property taxes, utilities, oil in the tank and similar fees based on your municipality. Responsibility varies.
- Other fees that can be paid by the seller such as: appraisals, inspections, paying the buyer's closing costs (if that has been negotiated as part of the deal).

Good faith or binder monies cannot be spent

If you are selling your home on your own and you accept a deposit from the buyer as a sign of "good faith," you are not allowed to spend it until the deal has closed. When working with a real estate attorney, he or she will hold that money in an escrow account until the transaction is complete. If the deal falls through, that money is typically returned unless there is a clause in the contract to the contrary.

Don't forget the little things

As soon as you are "in contract," meaning that both buyer and seller have signed a contract of sale, make your calls to your utilities and home insurance companies so they can be ready to switch or cancel service. Find out how many days' notice they need to make these changes. It's a small item on a very long "to do" list, but one that can be costly if left undone.

Keep your emotions out of the equation

Your home is special, and you've taken good care of it, when the inspector comes to check everything out it is best to stay neutral. Don't offer to take care of any repairs that come up during the inspection. Just be a quiet observer. You may not have to take care of some items and you don't want to promise a big pricey repair if it is not necessary. Don't get all hot and bothered that your home is being criticized. My advice is to wait for the entire report to come back and then you can negotiate wisely and from a strong position.

Inevitably, the inspector will find areas of the home that will need attending to like basement mold or a small leak stain on the ceiling. If you were the buyer wouldn't you want the seller to take care of that? Be open to what the seller requests and if it's reasonable, consider agreeing to it. If you are working with a real estate agent, they will be able to guide you more smoothly through repairs you should make versus what the buyer should take care of.

PART 2: WAYS TO GET MORE MONEY FOR YOUR HOME

CHAPTER 5

Successful, Yet Underused

During my years working in the contracting business and as a Licensed Real Estate Agent I have heard time and time again that the one thing a seller needs to do to attract buyers is to stage a home. Don't misunderstand, I don't mean just fill it with furniture… I mean using a designer's eye to bring rooms to life in the home you wish to sell. Professional accents such as window dressings, specific color and style of furniture that match the interior of your home's architectural touches. There are plenty of designers that do this for a living and can turn a room from simple and ordinary to appealing and exquisite. Once the home is properly staged have a professional photographer take gorgeous photos. I mean gorgeous photos.

Using these two suggestions will be why a property can sell faster and for a fair price even with similar competitive properties on the market. By taking advantage of a designer and a photographer's expertise, your home will surely stand out in the mind of the buyer. To some it may be an unwanted expense, but I guarantee that it will pay for itself. I would be happy to suggest a few designers and photographers if you'd like to investigate going that route. Even just to get an estimate and see samples of their work. In my opinion this is a successful yet underused way to sell your home in less time for more money.

Keep in mind the buyer's mindset and cultivate it in your listing

What is the real reason a buyer puts in an offer on a home? A real estate associate told me about a few homes in the same neighborhood on the market. Three of the houses were very similar and the fourth, while just as similar, had one big difference: a master bedroom suite. The real estate agent had taken his buyer around to show him all four homes. The three without the master suite were in the same price range. The fourth, lacked an updated exterior and was priced a bit higher.

The agent was sure his client would overlook this fourth house but he brought him through it regardless. The agent did not foresee the outcome that his client was so excited about the master suite with a jacuzzi in it that he told the agent to put in an offer that was close to the asking price right away.

At times it happens that way. Buyers sometimes fall in love with a unique feature of a house although the rest of the house seems ordinary. This real estate associate of mine had taken a lot of time showing his client many houses before this end result and he learned an important lesson: really get to know your client's desires. Don't assume it's the kitchen or backyard that will get them on board. It may be that jacuzzi in the master bath that turns out to be a person's deal maker.

Another colleague of mine took his clients out to find a rental for the summer. They spent a day viewing properties within walking distance to the beach. At the last home they came to in their price range the agent was getting frustrated. His client ended up putting an offer on this last house. Why you ask? Turns out it wasn't walking distance to the beach but it was close to the other side of the island and had a sitting area alongside a canal that faced west so they could see the sunset. Not everyone wants to be near the ocean during the summer. Instead they will choose to be in a quieter section with a pretty sunset.

When someone falls in love with a house there is little negotiation needed. They want the house and will pay to get it. Ultimately, when you are working with a real estate agent on the sale of your home my inclination is to encourage you to put a little extra time into developing or focusing on that little extra that might be its selling point. What is unique about your home and offers that something extra to a buyer? What brings you a bit more comfort or joy? What makes you smile about your home when you return to it from a long day at work? Once you determine that "thing," make sure it's highlighted in the listing and, if possible, attractively photographed.

CHAPTER 6

Better Marketing

There is so much to say about marketing home that the information could fill a book of its own. Even so, I will do my best to give you a sense of what your options may be as far as utilizing some marketing techniques.

Most home buyers find their home on the internet. While real estate agents are still contacted, most agents get a call from a buyer because of a home they saw online.

Not many buyers find their homes via newspaper ads although sometimes it is effective in a particular market. For instance, some upstate New York properties are advertised in Manhattan newspapers as second homes or vacation destinations for city-dwellers. Almost every home being sold today owes quite a bit of thanks to the internet. However, the internet is only one (albeit successful) piece of the advertising puzzle.

What you can do if you are selling on your own

Sellers, please beware, I see all too many people try to sell homes on their own and I constantly shake my head. How would anyone actually expect to sell what is most likely their biggest investment on their own only doing it for the first time? I wouldn't try to do surgery on myself and I don't suggest that you do either. Leave it to the professionals please and if you cannot then I suggest you find the best agent in your area and look at their listings and try to do the same if you can.

What you can expect your real estate agent to do for your property

Your Agent's Website

The more exposure your home gets the better the chance the information will reach your buyer. When choosing a real estate agent make sure to check out their website so you can see how they market their clients' properties. How attractive and appealing are the photos of the home? Do they provide any marketing statistics? Does the agent's site look professional and inviting? Well-designed websites tend to keep guests reading and clicking through to see more.

For my clients, I always go above and beyond what "the pack" seems to be doing. Most other agents join me in listing on MLS and every available real estate portal and directory. Because of my brokerage affiliation, I also market internationally which most agents do not have access to. As a rule, I always try to have professional staging and photography done. I also enlist drone video shoots and build out a small yet unique website for each property. The drone video shows prospective buyers the entire surrounding neighborhood both good and bad. Before all of this, I send in my crews to clean up and touch up the property after I do a "curb appeal analysis." Please take a look at www.KevinSimeRealEstate.com to see how I market different properties.

My level of dedication has me doing this usually at my own expense! I run a full-time social media campaign and I also have over 200 websites aimed at directing buyers into my pipeline which I then direct toward my different listed properties as well as properties that I have seen and I think are well maintained and are a good value.

 I pay for buyer leads as well from a major real estate portal. This choice brings me approximately 100 ready-to-buy clients every month usually with a pre-approval from a lender in hand. All of these different techniques make me a transaction machine and I don't know of any other realtor that does things the way I do. You will have a difficult time competing with that if you have a full- time job and are trying to sell your home on your own.

It is a numbers game and choosing a professional experienced agent will significantly increase your chances of selling your home. Talk with your agent about what sort of internet marketing they plan to do on your behalf and ask yourself if you could compete with that on your own; the decision seems very clear.

An educated and internet-savvy customer

With a few carefully constructed phrases, your next buyer could be viewing your home on the internet quickly. Sites like Zillow, Trulia, Realtor.com and MLSLI.com sort properties so that viewers can filter their search by neighborhood, price, number of bedrooms, square footage etc. You want to make sure your agent knows every fact about your home so they can lead buyers to it successfully. There was a time when real estate agents had a big book of homes for sale. The only way to see them was to pile into a car and go from house to house. Cell phones were not available and agents had to wait to get to the office to call and make an offer or type it up on the manual typewriter.

Nowadays, with our modern-day advances, a click of a mouse and a house can be viewed. Another click and the agent has been contacted and within a few e-mails, POOF the house has an offer! The process has been greatly accelerated and streamlined with technology. Since this is the case, make it a point to discuss with your agent the various ways he or she will market your home. Most listing agreements between agent and seller will detail marketing the home in general but be sure to ask if the home's information and photos will go onto social media. A tip to remember is when photos are being taken (by you, the agent or a professional) remove family photos or anything of a real personal nature that may sneak into a any photos.

Discuss with your agent other sites like Instagram, Twitter and Facebook so that you are comfortable with the exposure the home will get. If there is a floor plan of the home, ask that it be given out only upon request and not placed on the listing for just anyone to download. Also have current copies of your home insurance policies, survey's, elevation certificates, current tax info and any other pertinent data needed for a buyer to make an educated decision. You can be sure it will be requested as soon as you start to show your home.

Facebook, Instagram, Pinterest

These social media platforms are becoming more and more a standard in marketing properties. A particularly dramatic photo of the house may make a great "shareable" item and bring the home a lot of attention. This attention can grow around the neighborhood, the county and even the state! These platforms are terrific and free ways to advertise a home and the exponential value of a post is priceless.

Review the post with your agent carefully before posting so you get an idea of what's being put onto social media for all to see. Once a photo is posted it is very difficult to remove it.

Craigslist

Craigslist is another online site for selling anything including real estate. While Craigslist is an easy site to maneuver around, the better your pictures are and the more appealing the description, the better the responses you will receive. If you are doing this on your own, please be careful not to include the address; just post enough information to pique their interest. Make sure you meet prospective buyers in a safe location to make sure they are legitimate.

Before you spend time discussing the home, check and confirm that the buyer can show that they are pre-qualified for a mortgage that will more than pay for the cost of the listed property. Don't show a property to someone who just calls up on the phone. Working with Craigslist buyers can be successful, but one should proceed with caution.

An Individual website

I have worked with sellers who have created their own website for the home including elaborate descriptions of the property, professional photos, neighborhood details, links to school information, etc. It's a lot of work for those unfamiliar with creating a website but it can be a rewarding project. I've created multiple websites for my clients, and if anyone reading this would like my advice, please feel free to contact me. Agents usually have their own websites and can do this work easily.

(Visit www.KevinSimeRealEstate.com to see a sample.)

Mobile

An amazing boost for real estate agents was the invention of the cell phone. Within seconds an agent can search for a property and share it with a few clicks on their smartphone. Most agents have a mobile-friendly site or app that can be advertising your home, sending out floor plans, scheduling appointments, etc. Always make sure your agent is staying current with the latest marketing trends.

Snail mail is still a valuable advertising tool

It is true that e-mail and text are the preferred method of communication these days. In my experience, odds are that most of us will still read an attractively designed and informative real estate mailer. You may have heard the term "direct mail marketing." This simply means that the sender has gotten a list of owners and addresses. He or she has created an appealing flyer and mailed it out. These flyers or postcards often feature the agent's latest sale of a stunning home in the neighborhood with the words "JUST SOLD" across the front. The agent sending the flyer may want the community to know of a great home for sale just in case neighbors are looking for a way to get their friends or relatives into the community. The rates of success of these mailings do vary but it is still a viable way to let the world know your home is for sale.

Snail mail can highlight the positives of the property and provide a way for an interested party to book an appointment. This flyer/card is not super expensive; it is easy to design and worth the effort even in today's fast-paced world and real estate market.

Open Houses

Every weekend, except for the dead of winter, you might see balloons flying above signs with arrows that are stuck in the grass near the curbs. These signs might lead interested buyers and the curious to an open house. The day and time of the open house is listed on MLS so agents can prepare to stop by while out with their clients on a Saturday or Sunday.

Lately I'm even seeing "twilight" open houses which start around 5:00 pm and last until 7:00 pm just to offer every opportunity to have the home seen by prospective buyers. Another advantage to having a buyer's open house is that it allows many interested and/or curious buyers without agents as well as neighbors an opportunity to walk through the house without an appointment.

Neighbors are a good source to market toward as they might know someone looking to buy in their neighborhood or have a family member who is considering moving closer to them. When a home first goes on the market, agents do what is called a "brokers open house." At this event only other agents are invited to tour the property so they can run back and tell their buyers all about it. They tend to get a good turnout as agents usually get a reward for attending such as a nice meal, participation in a raffle, a swag bag, etc.

Open Houses (brokers or buyers) are still responsible for a good many offers on homes for sale. For the agent, it is a way to get more leads. Logistically even if a visitor to the open house is not interested in that specific property an agent could feasibly sign them up as a potential buyer and start taking them around to show them other properties. This is a veritable win-win all around. I am a strong believer that the seller should find something to do outside of the home for the duration of the open house(s) so the agent can do their job and/or network smoothly.

Homes being prepared for an open house event need to be shipshape: a freshly mowed lawn, carpets vacuumed, kitchen and bedrooms sparkling and tidied up, and a debris-free backyard. The cleaner you can make the house the better it presents. Make it shine! Agents schedule their open house days and times by looking up when other agents have set theirs. It helps those interested in any given community to get to see a selection of homes where the inventory and timing is grouped so it is in the interest of agents to work together this way. A crowd outside the door waiting to get in can be wonderful for generating excitement and perhaps a few offers on a listing. For those doing their own open house, you'll need to advertise it on social media and in and around the neighborhood a few days before. Have a few family members to help you so that you aren't there by yourself with a line of people waiting to get in. Put away your valuables and there is no harm done in spraying the rooms with a pleasing scent such as cinnamon or lemon.

How to throw a great open house

A typical open house should last one to two hours. This is plenty of time for interested buyers to get there and check out the listing. While you may have to spend a day or two preparing, it will be well worth it. My recommendation is to consider the following list of areas around the home to pay attention to:

- Trash cans should be cleaned, emptied and freshened with a pleasant scent.
- Odors emitted by pets or exotic cooking should be aired out or sprayed over where possible. Febreze is great for this and so is a scented candle.
- Dust everything.
- Wipe down the floors and vacuum all the rugs.
- Tidy up closets: pantries, linen, clothing and towel closets.
- Remove family photos and put up generic and attractive artwork.
- Sweep up leaves and make the effort to remove the dead blooms from any garden flowers or potted plants.
- Straighten up the garage.
- Place fresh flowers in a vase.
- Bake cookies.
- Make the beds.
- Organize children's bedrooms and toy areas.

- Clean the windows and, if need be, consider power-washing the home's exterior.
- If your neighbor has an eye-sore that will distract your listing's eye (such as overgrown bushes) offer to pay to have them clipped.
- If you are a smoker please remove all signs of the activity, ash trays etc.
- Clean or remove any kitty litter boxes or pet toys as well if possible.
- Vacuum and wipe off the boiler room. Wipe clean the boiler and hot water heater. This is done very rarely yet buyers look at this room quite seriously as to the age and condition of the units.

Take your open house up a notch

If your home is a resort-like property with a great entertaining space, you might consider offering something like a home party with a chef and music. Standardly I have cold water or Pellegrino as well as chocolate or doughnuts and coffee for my visitors. You want prospective buyers to linger and get comfortable in your home so give them some food for thought.

You may end up with a lot of nosey visitors who just want a free meal and an opportunity to peek inside your home. Frankly, there is nothing you can do about that as it comes with the territory.

CHAPTER 7

A Picture <u>IS</u> Worth A Thousand Words

High-quality photos are a must-have for selling a home. Truthfully, I can't even imagine selling a home without them. If these photographs have the right lighting, the right staging, show uncluttered and tastefully decorated rooms then your home has the potential of receiving a higher offer than a similar home with subpar photographs. Good photos should be a priority. Let's say you are going house hunting and have two properties to see. Would you choose the one that has photos that are slightly tilted, dimly lit and showing a kitchen sink with dishes still in it? I think not. I am fairly certain your choice would be a home that looks like it could be in a magazine. A common complaint I hear is that, "the photos look so much better than the house." With that fact in mind, it is seriously annoying to be out house shopping and visit a property because the photos look great but to your surprise, the house is nothing like the photos. This is a waste of everyone's time. Please try to be accurate in your descriptions and photography.

I doubt you will want to go into a home that looks unkempt and purchase it unless it is priced very low. If the photos show a home that has been well-cared for and that a homeowner has put in the time to show it off properly, odds are that is the home that will attract the most traffic. A proven strategy is taking several pictures of each room from different vantage points to determine which images seem the most attractive to the eye. Are your photos balanced and are the blinds level? Are the pillows placed correctly? Is there glare coming in through the windows? Meticulously review every corner of the photos to make sure you don't see toilet paper hanging from the holder in the bathroom or overflowing kitchen garbage in view. You do have the option of hiring a stager and/or a professional photographer who will create magazine-quality photos. It is not very expensive at all and well worth it.

However, here are some tips for taking winning photos:

Imagine you are entering a nice hotel room for the first time. How does it look and smell? That is the look and feel you are going after as you want it to appear clean and well thought out. First, clear the family photos and replace them with some simple decorations: a small clock or vase of flowers. Put any children's toys and animal bowls away. Spruce up the couch by purchasing some decorative pillows if you don't have them already. Window dressings should be neatly arranged and attractive.

For outdoor photos: don't take pictures on bright sunny days as it creates significant shadows. Photographing a listing on a semi-cloudy day results in balanced lighting. Mow the lawn, clip the hedges or tree overgrowth and sweep up any leaves. Remove your collection of lawn ornaments and consider planting some colorful flowers along walkways. Put down some fresh mulch around shrubs and trees. Wash the windows and power-wash the home exterior if applicable. More and more homeowners are hiring photographers with drones who can take aerial videos of the neighborhood. Drone aerial video footage can show how close your home is to shopping, schools, parks, the ocean and local commuting roads. Make sure your drone video highlights anything worthwhile close to your home. These videos, while not totally necessary, add a wow factor to what are normally ordinary pictures. Choosing to utilize this service will make your property stand out from the rest.

Photographers can also record a video walk-thru of the property with narration if desired. This can be particularly handy for those potential buyers who are from out of state and are looking for a property; they can imagine walking through the home even if they aren't able to do so in person. A video such as this may peak a buyer's interest in the listing over and above photographs and they may decide to come to your home in person. Why not increase your odds? These techniques are standard fare for my clients as a realtor or consultant.

CHAPTER 8

Up Your Curb Appeal

This term has been around a long time: "curb appeal." Simply it means: how attractive does your home look when pulling up to the curb? Does it wow you and make you stop in your tracks? If not, does it make you want to keep going? I truly feel the first view of a home from the sidewalk or street for a buyer is of the ultimate importance. If the curb appeal fills a buyer with excitement, then you've almost won the battle. If the lack of polish/appeal makes your buyer squirm you may have already lost them before they have even gotten through the front door.

Make that first look impressive: sidewalk, walkway, front door, windows, landscaping and anything else that is found in the front of your home should be straightened up. Have a neighbor stand across the street from your home and ask them for feedback. A home that has been cared for on the outside will tell a buyer that the rest of the house has been cared for as well. Don't disappoint your potential buyers. Once they enter the home, let them see that you've maintained the interior as well. You may actually get an offer that is close or even above your asking price for investing a few hundred dollars and a few hours of work.

The front door and entrance

The front door and entrance should continue "wowing" your buyer. Look carefully at the doorknobs, doorknocker, paint job and any decorative window or door frame. Are they appealing or is there paint chipping? Is anything in need of a washing? Does the door and door knob open and close properly? How is the lock? Does it look secure? Are the address numbers neatly presented? Is the mailbox old and rusty?   These can be very inexpensive repairs and replacements, but they are well worth the effort.

Also, if you have a screen door, inspect it for holes. Make sure it closes smoothly and securely latches itself. Look carefully and don't be afraid to really inspect these areas with an objective eye. Wash, repair and replace what is necessary.

Windows

All windows should be thoroughly cleaned and free of any dirt or debris in the window wells. All windowpanes should be free of paint on the glass. They should open and close easily with one hand preferably. All window locks / closures should be in working order. Window screens and storm windows should also be clean and operational as well.

Doors

All interior and exterior doors should open and close properly. Doors should have working doorknobs that latch properly and have matching style as well. I immediately notice when a home has several different non matching door knob and hinge styles all over the place. It is sloppy and careless, and it is an inexpensive easy fix that has a huge impact and shows there is a homeowner that cares about their property.

Floors

Floors should be cleaned and shined if not completely refinished with fresh polyurethane etc. A great trick for squeaky floors is to pour some talc powder on the squeaky area. The talk usually stops the squeak and you can sweep up the excess. Steam-clean carpets, grout and upholstered furniture. Don't go into any costly replacements of flooring unless there are any unsafe areas that truly need addressing or tiles that are loose and or unsightly that detract from the beauty of the property. Please replace any missing grouting from floor or wall tiles.

Backyard

While the backyard is often the last thing your buyers will see, make your backyard appealing and comforting. They may be pretty worn out by the time they get there. Make your backyard welcoming and inviting for them to see. If Fido dug holes or killed areas of grass then fix them and re-seed the area. Hot tubs and pools should be secure with covers and be well-maintained and operational. Clean the patio furniture, replace worn out chairs and add planted flowers around walkways. Place some bird seed in that old bird feeder...anything to make it feel like home.

Looks mean a lot

Let's say your roof is nearly new and the appliances have been updated. Add that the floors are sparkling, and the kitchen is newly renovated. Keep in mind that if the exterior of the home is worn out, outdated and neglected you may find that buyers will ignore your home as well.   Interior work matters but so does the exterior appearance of the home. One of my personal favorites is when a seller has recently installed a new roof, but they neglected to do the garage roof as well. It is super clear that a complete job is a foreign concept and instantly has me looking for other short cuts they might have taken.

CHAPTER 9

Tips On Staging

It is a fact that staged homes command a higher price compared to non-staged homes. At times a properly staged home can create such excitement that it helps bring forth offers well over your asking price. Why not increase your chances of success with such an investment in staging? There are 2 types of staging that I refer to. One is to hire a professional to come in and bring in new furniture and artwork etc. The other is to have a pro come in and rearrange your existing furnishings. The second option is much less costly.

Ideas to share

Before you make any big changes to your home interior have it cleaned from top to bottom. Dust around moldings, light fixtures, countertops, furniture trims/edges and shelving. Make everything shine while clearing clutter. Go through rooms and remove items: books, crowded countertop displays and bric-a-brac. When you think you're done? Go through it all again. I cannot stress enough to really empty the rooms while placing simple items like small vase accents filled with flowers. This is a great time to start packing up non essential possessions, place all the non day to day items you plan to keep in boxes, label them and put them in the garage ready to be moved to your new home. A buyer will understand boxes in a garage but will have a hard time visualizing a house that is filled with clutter.

Remove unnecessary furniture so that rooms look less crowded. There is a balance of course so don't declutter so much that the rooms look bare. For example, add a rocking chair to an empty bedroom corner. Are you working on a puzzle or quilt? Please put it away or find a spot that you can call a "hobby room." Inspect the home's plumbing: a perpetually running toilet and a leaky faucet may be things that you have gotten used to. These issues will stick out like a sore thumb to a new pair of eyes. Do you have wild colors painted on the walls in any of the rooms or bedrooms? If so then do yourself a favor and repaint them something more neutral such as off-white or grey.

Future buyers will struggle to imagine your rooms in a softer color, and they will always recall negatively that house with the orange walls so please paint them before it becomes a speed bump. It is a good suggestion to put away for the open house any overtly religious items, statues, wall crosses, etc. The home should be appreciated for its beauty and not it's political or religious leaning. Your personality and beliefs should stay out of a showing. No one needs to know which religion or sports team you are affiliated with. Organize closets and pantries and try to think like a very important guest is coming for a weekend visit.

Stage each room and closet so that the house looks balanced and clean. A staged room next to a busy/cluttered room is going to be unattractive and work against your sale. Walk through your home and take note of how well it is lit. While most showings occur during daylight hours, keep in mind, for dark and gray days to make sure there is enough lighting (artificial or natural) in place to make the rooms look bright and inviting. Make sure all light bulbs are working and are the same size and color if possible.

Check the attic and basement to make sure the lighting is in good working order in both locations.   Make sure your light bulbs are all the same size and shape. Uniformity makes a big difference to the viewing eye and overall aesthetic! Do all of the closet doors close and latch properly? Make sure they hang straight and do not rub against the floor. Clean up after the pets including in the backyard. When you are in doubt you can always hire an inspector that will walk through the house looking for areas that need to be improved as you put the house on the market. Some will be able to do the repair themselves or provide names of professionals you can contact on your own. I tend to do a lot of that for my clients and I frequently send over my own team to clean and paint so we are ready to show.

CHAPTER 10

Recommended Home Improvements

I sometimes refer to myself as the "remodeling real estate agent." By all means groan away, but with my feet in both worlds I have a trained and unique eye for what should and should not be repaired in order to sell. I can confidently tell you whether or not a repair is worth the effort and what the actual cost may be. Please understand that while some improvements are a good idea, they may not be worth the dollars invested. If your bathroom is outdated, you may consider gutting it and remodeling it but only if the other bathrooms are new.

It is possible that after that effort and expense that the new owners may not like the colors and fixtures you've chosen, and it may mean you end up not getting back what you invested into it. Something else to consider is even though more and more bathtubs are being removed, many buyers still like a tub (especially if they have young children). Leave the tub alone and skip the remodeling and instead put that money into something else like the curb appeal or a damp basement. Your buyer is going to be hesitant purchasing a home that has existing problems to attend to right after closing. If you are selling on your own at the very least call in an inspector to see what may be mandatory repairs or improvements for your specific home.

Here are areas around the home that need to be examined, preferably by an expert, before selling your home:

The wiring / Electrical Service

I choose this area first for safety's sake. Take the time to examine your home's wiring, outlets and ground fault circuits. Check to make sure you don't have any overloaded outlets. How well are the outlets spaced out? Make sure wires and surge suppressor strips aren't stretched across the floors. Changing out all the outlets and wall switch-plates with crisp and uniform new ones is a small expense that provides a huge return in terms of aesthetics. This small edit can be a valuable selling point! These days, a current 200-amp electrical panel is always a highlight and spoken about at almost every showing.

The plumbing

Check that all toilets operate, turn off quickly and fill properly after flushing. Faucets should all work and shouldn't drip. The water pipes shouldn't rumble when the water is turned on. I know this is obvious but water shouldn't be brown or smell at all, I have seen it many times in my career. A professional grade water filter connected to the house main sends filtered water to every water source inside the home. It is not expensive, and it is a great selling point.

Heating and cooling

Check that the radiators are working, and the covers are on them (if applicable). Make sure they are clean and dust-free. Review ceiling, wall and floor vents where relevant. Be certain they are working and replace them if need be. Window unit air conditioners should be sitting nicely in the windows and their filters should be cleaned. Central air vents should all be functioning properly. Having your ducts cleaned is an inexpensive and very nice selling option to put forth. Doing this shows you care about your home inside and out and want to sell a meticulously cared for home to your prospective buyer. Do you have a 50-year-old thermostat in your home? Replace it ASAP. It is an easy fix for under $100

Odors / Mold

Get a fresh nose involved to smell out odors. Have a friend walk through and give it the smell test. Just in case there was a leak and smelly mold behind the wall or even worse…a dead rodent. Find it before your buyer does! Speaking of mold, most states are enacting serious mold laws and it is something everyone should be aware of. Just like the recently enacted EPA lead laws, mold is now being held to the same legal standard and rightly so. Mold can be toxic and life threatening to humans. I know in New York, lawmakers basically took the entire lead law and added the word mold in its place. Inspectors are savvy to this fact and I have seen home sales tied up in mold testing and remediation several times already. It can be quite costly and to put it plainly, the old days of pouring bleach on it are over. If you know you have mold or suspect a mold problem, get ahead of it before you decide to sell.

Kitchen and Appliances

Stainless steel appliances are all the rage. Hear me out when I say if you don't have them then don't upgrade your present appliances. The buyer will want to choose their own. Just have the appliances clean and sparkling. A little elbow grease goes a long way. Clean the inside of all of the appliances: fridge, stove, microwave and dishwasher. If you have a garbage disposal, consider a freshener for it.

Something to consider in the kitchen would be the option to add a new backsplash if the one you have shows wear and tear. Maybe you could consider adding a fresh new faucet to replace a worn one?

New cabinet hardware: handles, knobs and hinges as well as simple cabinet door adjustments are inexpensive improvements that can bring up appearances of older cabinetry and spruce up the kitchen just by adding them!

Bathrooms

In most bathrooms little changes can make a big difference. The addition of a new toilet seat, an accent floor rug, polishing up the faucets and the scrubbing the tub. Look for mold in the corners and check any windows for wear and tear. A coat of paint will definitely freshen any bathroom up. Make sure to really clean the grout between tiles and remove/replace any old caulking in the shower corners. Have your plumber check to see if your shower water pressure is as powerful as possible. I am not a fan of a weak shower and many buyers feel the same way!

Roof and gutters

Stand across the street and view the roof for any loose or missing shingles. This is a repair worth doing so as not raise any flags that there might be more issues with the roof. Don't give the buyer any reason to offer a rock-bottom price because a missing shingle caused them to worry. Clean any leaves or debris from the gutters. I also suggest cleaning the actual face of the gutters. Over time the petroleum ingredients from roofing shingles tend to stain white gutters with a dark stain that often forms a tiger stripe. This is easily cleaned with some elbow grease and a cleaning product like Simple Green.

Deal Killers

If you know that you have made any major improvements over the years and not filed the proper plans and permits with your local municipality/building department you aren't fooling anyone! Don't think for a second in this day and age that your buyer's attorney, title company or mortgage company will not find an illegal deck or non-permitted gas fireplace. The only person looking foolish will be you. Recently, I had a beautiful home sale go sour because of these same issues. My clients had an illegal deck and an illegal gas fireplace. They refused to go through the time and expense to file the proper documents years ago when they installed them, and they also refused to legalize them prior to listing their home. Of course, these issues came up as the closing approached and spooked the buyer into backing out of a perfectly good home last minute. The buyer's exact words to me were, "What else are they hiding?"

Now the sellers who had looked at dozens of new properties could not move forward with their plans to move on. In the end it was a total waste of everyone's time and money not to mention really bad karma in my opinion! The buyer lost the money he spent on a lawyer and a home inspection. The seller wasted a ton of time (mine and theirs) looking at properties that they cannot buy until they sold their home. The seller's attorney is not going to do a second transaction for free which also cost them. As a result, I had to remarket the home, arrange more open houses and show the sellers more properties once they were able to buy a home. All of this was a major (and yet avoidable) expense for me and for them.

Something to remember is that Building Department fees can be double the original price when you decide to go ahead with legalizing after the fact. Imagine how much time, energy, money and good will could have been saved had my clients chose to do the right thing from the beginning! One might say they tripped over a dollar to pick up a nickel. My advice is to please avoid this costly mistake.

What do buyers want?

To summarize this briefly, buyers want a home that has the important items either new or recently updated. This way they don't have to make any changes right away and everything should be in working order. Buyers want an easy to maintain property inside and out and a home that has been cared for. Keep in mind the little things like having the manuals for the appliances readily available to the buyers goes a long way. Most buyers do not want a really big gardening headache. Instead they prefer areas that are easy to tend to like shrubs and evergreens. If you are going to have big ticket items like hot tubs and in-ground pools, they really need to show and operate perfectly. A new owner does not want to start having problems with a luxury amenity that isn't working properly. One unique idea I love to suggest is to buy a one-year home warranty like American Home Shield to gift to your home buyer. It shows you are willing to stand behind your product!

PART 3: FOR THE BUYERS

CHAPTER 11

Answers To The Most Popular Questions

One of the perks of my job is helping my clients find and purchase their dream home. I am particularly fond of first-time home buying transactions. For new buyers your agent needs to help educate you and guide you along the way. I want to make sure you understand every step in the process. A good agent will look for clues from what their client shares about where they want to live. He or she will also learn from you what your budget is and what your timeline and hopes are. A good agent has to listen equally as much as they speak.

If you are going to go out into the world to buy your home yourself, it is possible but why would you do that? You can search for listings on the internet and call to make arrangements with different listing agents. Something I need to share with you is that the broker or listing agent does not owe you anything. Their fiduciary commitment is to their client the seller and not you the buyer. This can be a precarious situation as to who exactly is looking out for your best interests in any given transaction.

While you think you are being shown a home by an agent who will look out for you it is not likely. If you are already aware of this then that is great. If you weren't aware of this dynamic, then I am glad you are reading this guide. Please make sure you highlight this: <u>if you go view a home on your own with the agent who is representing the seller be certain that they are not looking out for you</u>. Now that I have said this, let me go through what a buyer needs to look out for.

Why are you buying a house?

What category do you fit in? Are you a first-time buyer or are you looking to upsize or downsize? You really need to know why you are certain you want to buy. Are you familiar enough with interest rates to know how present loan figures and numbers will apply to you and your budget? Do you know enough about your credit score to be able to borrow enough money for the home you plan to purchase?

Know your reasons for buying and make sure you can handle the realities of home ownership. How much land do you want to maintain? Do you plan to add to your family and have more children? Do you one day plan to have in-laws move in or would you ever hire an au pair? Make a list of what you wish your family and your home's future will look like so it can aid your search productively and not be a waste of time. You don't want to be disappointed because you are declined the mortgage. Nor do you want to make that purchase only to find that you've neglected to allow room for grandparents to move in to babysit. Try to look at the whole picture.

What is involved financially with home ownership?

I had a client who was ready to purchase a house but was not very savvy about the big picture of homeownership. Their family and their friends were renters making them the first in their circle to make the move towards homeownership. When we sat down to review listings, my client was unaware about the expenses that go along with being a homeowner beyond the mortgage and insurance. I explained that homes owe taxes to the various municipalities it resides in, i.e., sewer taxes, water taxes and school taxes for the upkeep of the district. It was a real eye-opener to them for what they were in for. Once the shock wore off, they were ready to pursue homes that fit in their budget mortgage-wise and they understood what funds were needed for these ancillary financial obligations. If you are in a similar circumstance, visit your local town hall to see what taxes are placed on properties in the area or consider calling myself or a real estate attorney for a consultation and a list of all the outside expenses that come along with a typical purchase.

How does a house work?

It's one thing to purchase a car without knowing exactly how the engine works. But it's another thing completely to be a homeowner and not at least try and understand how a home works. There are so many moving parts to a home and the more you can learn about it the bigger position of strength you are in. Knowledge that helps you with a routine home repair will go a long way toward having a pleasant and manageable homeownership experience and make you feel more independent.

Please don't misunderstand, I truly feel that there are areas that should be left to professionals. These include electrical and plumbing work.   This work is required to adhere to industry and safety standards.   Roofing is another hands-off area best left to a professional.   Alternatively, there are plenty of tasks/projects you can and should take on if you are handy and willing: landscaping, minor plumbing repair, painting, removing carpets, power-washing the pavers and siding, staining the deck and learning how to make other small repairs around the home. Local hardware stores offer "do it yourself" classes and there is a wealth of information in internet videos on how to do simple tasks around the house. To summarize my thoughts on this, get knowledgeable about your home so that you can keep up with all of the workings within it from top to bottom. You could save yourself a lot of unnecessary bills with what you can do yourself. The major bonus here is also the "pride of homeownership" and being aware that you are taking care of your most valuable investment on your own.

Do you plan to live in your home for 20 years?

This is a question worth considering as you go about the house-hunting process. Perhaps you are single and want to make this purchase now and get yourself set up. However, circumstances may change, and you may find a partner or spouse within a few years and, in turn, need to find a place you both can agree on. Alternatively, maybe you have just started a family and have one child and you are undecided on expanding your family. Details such as these should factor into the home you are looking for. It also has an impact on the mortgage you take out.

Do you work with one realtor or several different ones, and what is the rule of thumb?

Here is how it can go. You are ready to start looking and have a neighborhood in mind. You are confident of your affordable price range and you know the number of bedrooms you need. You have an idea of how much land you would like your property to have and it is clear the school district you want. For your next step you research the internet and find some homes to check out. Turns out each one has a different agent with a different contact number. You have some options: contact an experienced Real Estate Agent that specializes with buyers, a "buyer's agent". How you ask? You can get referrals from friends or business associates for an agent, or ask your attorney. Believe it or not, many agents refuse to work with buyers as it tends to be harder work for an agent. I enjoy this type of real estate and tend to focus on it primarily.

Truthfully, any agent within the area can show you available properties. They will also find out if these listings are actually still on the market. The agent you choose will run each listing and check out how it is shown and make an appointment. You don't have to call each agent that is listed on any property listing. You are better off having one trusted agent to do this work for you. Do you really want to have to call back three or four different agents to confirm appointments? Having each agent give you his or her opinion of the market could be varied and overwhelming.

Your other option is to work with one experienced agent who will keep it all organized for you. Please be as forthcoming and honest about what you are searching for. Giving an agent a bunch of maybe this or maybe that is not only frustrating; it is also counterproductive and confusing to everyone. A great agent will get to know you and your specific wants and needs. A great agent also has their ear to the ground and hears about new listings sometimes before they go out to the public. After getting to know your wants, an agent can then search with enough confidence to then be able to find other listings that suit your needs. Perhaps even your IDEAL listing! Consider it. It costs you nothing to work with a buyer's agent as the majority of all listings are placed on MLS and have a commission percentage built in to them automatically that pays for both agents. Where else can you have an industry expert work for you for free? I can't think of another industry that works like this. Why would you go to court without a lawyer or even worse, go to court and use your opponent's lawyer? Please rethink working with a qualified experienced agent in the buying or selling process.

How many homes should you look at before deciding?

If you are working with an agent who knows exactly what you are looking for: number of bedrooms, bathrooms, desired neighborhood, etc. you should not be looking at more than six or eight homes. Working with an agent means that a large chunk of your time is saved by having them search for the ideal properties, so you are not wasting your time. Let them do their job. If you are serious about buying, you should have a mortgage commitment and know what price range you can work with. In this scenario, with your readiness, every house you look at should be a real contender.

If your agent shows you a list of 50 houses to look at, be suspicious why they haven't whittled them down to the best of the best. If I send someone a list of 50 houses, it is simply because they are being vague and refusing to be open and honest with me about their wants or intentions. Sure, it is possible that there are just a lot of houses in that community that matches your criteria, but that result should make you pause and ask is there reason for a large inventory of homes on the market? Why is everyone leaving?

How many times do you go back to see a home before you decide to put in an offer?

Remember that a great house at a great price will not last long. If you see the house you really, really like (it may happen after seeing five houses or it may happen after seeing one) let the agent know. He or she may encourage you to put in an offer right away. It costs nothing to put in an offer and you are not committed to purchase just by making an offer. If the purchase depends on another family member's approval, make that second visit ASAP. Without a firm offer, that house will continue to be shown and your delay may have you lose out on the property entirely.

In short, see it the first time and, if necessary, a second time. This should really be enough. If you really like a home, please take pictures or video to help you make a smart and informed decision. If you love a house and it is priced right, odds are there are other buyers who feel the same way. Get your offer in quickly and beat the competition!

What to look for at an open house?

An open house is a wonderful way to get your first initial look at a house without the pressure of making an appointment. It is wise to go with your agent, but you can also go on your own. When you enter the home the agent who is hosting the open house will ask you to sign in with an e-mail and a phone number. He or she may also ask if you are working with an agent. If you are working with an agent, that agent knows enough not to pursue you as a client. If you are not working with an agent, they will want to continue to be in touch. Their goal is to discuss the house in question and/or to show you additional homes.

During the open house, be sure to take any flyers you can to keep track of the houses you've seen. Make notes as you go, write down your questions and if permitted take your own photos (but please ask permission). Don't go to too many open houses in one day since it will overwhelm you. Make sure to get a bite to eat in between homes so that you keep up your energy. Look out for any red flags such as smells or areas that you are not allowed to inspect. Every part of the house should be available for viewing. Walk the backyard and see what is around you. Are there trees, a basketball hoop in the neighbor's yard, barking dogs, etc.? Go down to the basement and ask to peek in the attic as that is where many problems tend to hide. Turn on the faucets and showers and pay attention to any staircases and railings as they rent to take a beating over time. Check out any stonework. Is it neat or crumbling? Do the walls need to be painted? Is there central air and an updated furnace? Are there newer kitchen appliances?

Make a note as to what you will want to change and update. Don't think that you'll remember this when you get home. You won't. Make all your notes at the time of the open house. You will be thankful you did.

How to even begin to put in an offer?

I hope that when you get to the point of putting in an offer that you will have either a real estate agent or a real estate attorney working for you. This is a very delicate process that requires an experienced professional. Your offer may be way off target. It could be based on misinformation and be either too low or too high and you may lose out on a great deal. Why would you take the chance? All I can say is if you insist on putting in your own offer, there is a fine line between being too low or too high.

Why you should consider getting pre-qualified for a mortgage?

There are several reasons why you should consider getting pre-qualified for a mortgage. This way you know ahead of time what price range you can afford. You will also learn how long you will be paying off the mortgage and having this in place makes you a more viable/valuable buyer. Obtaining a mortgage commitment means you are a serious buyer and a seller may not even entertain your offer without one.

I know that in my office specifically, an offer is not even looked at without a mortgage commitment or pre-approval letter. For this, I recommend making an appointment with a representative at the bank you do your business at. I would also be sure to get a second opinion. Even though it is problematic to send in all your information and paperwork a second time, it is a big loan and a small variation in percentage points can cost you thousands over the typical 30 year lifespan of a loan.

Choose wisely, you as the buyer pay for any home inspections

This is one of those "just for your information" tips. Once you lock in on a house and make an offer which is accepted, it should always be contingent upon the inspection. This inspection is paid for by the buyer and that is so you <u>ONLY</u> make the offer on the one house you really want. An inspection can run between $500 and $1,000 and since you don't want to pay for any more than one… ok two if the first one falls through. Keep in mind an inspection is the best money you'll ever spend. I have included a sample inspection at the end of this guide so you can have a feel for what to expect when that time comes.

Even if you are buying a home on your own you still need a real estate attorney

If you are buying a home on your own, without an agent, and you've gotten to the time of signing contracts, you MUST have a real estate attorney to review the contract. In my area, their fee may be approximately $1000 - $1,500 and that will cover all negotiations. They will review every detail and make sure you aren't being bamboozled by either a FSBO owner or an unscrupulous agent. This is a must. If you need a real estate attorney referral, I can confidently recommend some of most highly qualified attorneys in the business.

Negotiating the price

In most financial transactions of a home purchase, a price is negotiable. The exceptions are bank- owned or foreclosures. Sellers almost always leave wiggle room in their sale price. Buyers do the same and leave wiggle room in their offer. It's the agents who really earn their commission here when they work for you the buyer and assist you to get a property at the lowest price possible. Your agent may have been able to have the seller repair the roof, fix the fence or replace windows. An agent with expertise knows where they can ask for something or when to accept or give in to something else. This is where a deal becomes unique. A buyer who is working on their own tends to get overwhelmed at this point, realizing they are out of their element.

What happens after the offer is accepted?

Things start moving quickly as a mortgage commitment standardly has an expiration date. You may have a home to sell or the seller has another home they are purchasing. As a result, everyone must get their own ducks in a row. Your agent will advise you every step of the way from: getting a mortgage, taking care of your present living situation, i.e., notifying a landlord and utility companies of your impending move. Your agent will arrange to get the home inspected and negotiate all the demands so that a contract can be signed. Normally, once the contract is signed, the closing occurs within two to three months from that date. Your agent or real estate attorney should keep up with this timeline and advise you along the way.

Keep in mind, more often than not, you will need to pay most of the closing costs as buyer. These costs often include title search (which ensures that there are no liens or outstanding permits on the property), home insurance, movers, etc. Once the closing date is set, you will need to transfer utilities to your name, or open new accounts, i.e. fuel delivery, water bills, electricity, etc.

PART 4: HOW I CAN HELP YOU

Congratulation on getting this far into my book! It shows that you are serious about learning all you can about buying or selling your home. It also demonstrates that you appreciate that small changes can mean a satisfying and profitable property transaction. Also important in the whole process is the knowledge of how to deal with the offer that comes in or goes out.

Remember, when you work with an agent, they receive all offers and can help you choose which ones are legit and which ones are just "testing the market." Agents can also advise you as to which offers to consider and which to disregard. Knowing this can save you big headaches and put more money in your pocket in the end. Let the agent do the heavy lifting of offer/buyer analysis.

As your agent, with my extensive experience, I can help you choose which offer will be the best fit for you and your needs. I have the ability to discern if the buyer has to sell a property as a precursor to having the money to buy your home. I can make sure your tax information is correct or instruct you on how to grieve your taxes if I feel it is necessary. I can also review your home and determine that you have all the permits you need for changes made to your home over time. I also call the mortgage brokers attached to offers as well. Sometimes, a buyer has a pre qualification or a pre approval and their finances have not been properly vetted making them an unsuitable buyer.

A real estate agent earns their commission

This scenario is common: a FSBO owner puts their house on the market for what they feel is a very fair price. In fact, the price is very fair, but no offers come in. What happens next? The FSBO immediately drops the price out of fear. As a result of this the house hunters' whispers begin about the home having something wrong with it. Why else would the price be lowered? The fears now prevent more buyers from coming to tour the home. The seller, once again, reduces the price even further in a panic.

Working with a realtor could have prevented all the above from happening. Had a real estate agent been used in this scenario, a completely different outcome would have resulted. A good realtor would have known that the original price the owner suggested would not work because of market fluctuation. They may have cautioned the owner to wait a bit for the market to turn. They may have even suggested that a simple home update be done. An experienced agent may propose a strategy of offering a lower price than the seller suggested to create flurry of attention inciting many buyers come that could create a bidding war. Most importantly an agent will help you make more educated decisions.

A solid agent will aid you in making experienced suggestions about your property overall and help you hold your ground when it is needed during the sale process. In most cases, your real estate agent can negotiate well enough to cover their own commission in the asking price. Your agent will know more about your prospective buyer in many cases. In their experience they just notice more than you will. Your agent also may get some inside information from the buyer's agent. Maybe the buyer is moving from another location and is in a bit of hurry and motivated. Your agent will know when to jump at an offer or when to dig in and wait it out. Your agent will know how much to divulge during a showing and what not to share. An innocent comment about the neighbors being noisy may be just conversational on your part but end up being a deal breaker for the buyer. Be vague when answering questions about why you're moving. That may be the buyer's way of sneaking information out of you. Prepare to have a handy response, like you want to move closer to relatives.

This is my promise to you. Work with me and I will ensure that you get as much for your home as you can possibly get. If you are in the other position (needing to buy a home) I promise the same successful result for you. Don't wait until you are in the middle of a big home issue (structural, legal or otherwise) which can arise during a real estate transaction to call in an expert. This book is a labor of love for me: to present as many money and time-saving tips to as many readers out there as possible.

Eye openers

In the following pages I have included a summary of a recent home inspection report that was generously provided to me by my friends at Safe Harbor Home Inspections. I would urge all buyers as well as any seller to read it through to see the extent of, and detail in, a good home inspection. For a seller, please look at this as a checklist for getting your home, mechanically, ready for sale. For a buyer, please use this as a checklist of items/issues to look for and questions to ask.

Having completed my book, I hope you can now go confidently and wisely into any real estate transaction with more knowledge and added confidence. <u>Please remember that I do not recommend using anyone other than a competent licensed professional for any and all matters regarding your home.</u>

 Good luck in your real estate endeavors and please feel free to reach me directly for any questions or advice:

Kevin Sime

87

Licensed Real Estate Salesperson

516-697-1433

KevinSimeRealEstate@gmail.com

ADDENDUM

Inspection Report

Prepared for: **Mr. and Mrs. Jones**

Property Address:
123 School Street
Any Town NY 11777
Prepared by:

Safe Harbor Inspections Inc.
Home Inspector License NY 16000008389

Table of Contents

7 STRUCTURAL COMPONENTS
8 PLUMBING SYSTEM
9 ELECTRICAL SYSTEMS
10 HEATING
11 AIR CONDITIONING
12 GENERAL INFORMATION ABOUT THE PROPERTY
13 GENERAL RECOMMENDATIONS
14 HOME WARRANTY INFORMATION
15 ITEMS/COMPONENTS NOT INSPECTED
16 HOME INSPECTION EXPECTATIONS
17 New York State Standards of Practice and Code of Ethics
18 FINAL WALK THROUGH CHECK LIST
Invoice
Back Page
Agreement

Safe Harbor Inspections Inc. Jones
123 School Street
Date: 10/29/2019
Start Time: 09:00 AM
Stop Time 12:00 PM Report ID: 123 School Street

Property:
123 School Street
Any Town NY 11777
Customer: Mr. and Mrs. Jones
Real Estate Professional:
Age of structure (according to the seller): Over 25 Years
Client Is Present: Yes
Rain in past 24 hours: No
Pre-Inspection Agreement
executed: On-Line before inspection, Hard copy before
inspection
Occupancy condition of house: OCCUPPIED WITH
FURNITURE
Present at Inspection: Buyer, Listing Agent, Buyers Agent,
Seller

Authorized persons to receive report: Buyer, Buyers Agent

Important, please read:

THIS IS NOT A TECHNICALLY EXHAUSTIVE INSPECTION: You are advised that you can purchase a technically exhaustive inspection and that a fee for this type of inspection could be $5,000.00 or more, depending on the home. The fee is so much more because we will need to retain other specialists as necessary to prepare a technically exhaustive report. Destructive testing (opening some walls and ceilings for example) will be required and will necessitate the seller's approval. A request in writing for this service must be accompanied by a 50% deposit required to commence this inspection. If you wish this enhanced inspection please notify the Safe Harbor and another inspection date will be scheduled after an appropriate pre-inspection agreement is entered into.

Unless you purchase this Technically Exhaustive Inspection you cannot and must not assume that we will report on all defects. Therefore, you cannot and must not base all of your practical negotiations on the results of this inspection. Nor should you base all of your budgeting for future repairs solely on this inspection, because THIS IS NOT A TECHNICALLY EXHAUSTIVE INSPECTION.

This report can only be relied upon by the original paying client of Safe Harbor Inspections Inc unless a separate Inspection Agreement is entered into with Safe Harbor Inspections Inc. In order to make this report as meaningful and as easy as possible to read and understand, only the items that were found to be noteworthy during the inspection are included in this report. Therefore, items that were found to be in acceptable condition are not mentioned and are not included in this report.

Please note, the advice and services of specialists will be recommended for many conditions described in the report. All specialists must be licensed and qualified to provide the recommended service. Use of an unlicensed or unqualified contractor will likely result in poor quality work, aggravation and higher costs in the end.

Comment Key or Definitions:

**Safe Harbor Inspections Inc.
Jones
123 School Street**

The following categories will appear as a component of each comment. These categories are intended to help you understand the findings of the inspection.

I: (Informational) This category includes comments provided as general recommendations and for your information. NI: (Not Inspected) This item was not inspected and the reason for not inspecting it will be stated. M: (Maintenance) The item, component needs general maintenance or repair/replacement. P: (Priority) This is a priority or safety item that should be done ASAP.

**Safe Harbor Inspections Inc.
Jones 123 School Street**

1. EXTERIOR

The inspector shall inspect: the exterior wall coverings, flashing, and trim. All exterior doors. Attached decks, balconies, stoops, steps, porches, and their associated railings. The eaves, soffits and fascia's where accessible from the ground level. The vegetation, grading, surface drainage, and retaining walls on the property when any of these are likely to adversely affect the building. Walkways, patios, and driveways leading to dwelling entrances. Describes the exterior wall covering.

The inspector is not required to inspect: Screening, shutters, awnings, and similar seasonal accessories. Fences. Geological, geotechnical, or hydrological conditions. Recreational facilities. Outbuildings. Sea walls, break walls, and docks. Erosion control and earth stabilization measures.

Items

1.0 DECKS AND PORCHES (TOP SIDE)
Comments: Maintenance/Repairs
1.1 DECK STRUCTURE (UNDERSIDE)
Comments: Maintenance/Repairs
DECK GUARD RAILS LOOSE: The deck guardrails are loose. This is a safety hazard and should be corrected by a deck contractor or carpenter.
AGED WOOD ON DECK: The wood on the deck is cracking and splitting due to age. Although the wood is structurally sound, splinters are common. At some point you may want to consider a new floor surface.
1.0 Item 1(Picture)
(1) DECK JOIST HANGERS MISSING: The deck should have joist hangers to properly support the joists. It is recommended that these hangers be installed by a carpenter to ensure structural integrity of the deck.

Safe Harbor Inspections Inc. Jones
123 School
1.2 DRAINAGE AROUND FOUNDATION
Comments: Maintenance/Repairs
1.1 Item 1(Picture)

(2) DECK LAG BOLTS MISSING:
The deck should have lag bolts installed. These bolts ensure a solid connection of the deck to the house. It is recommended that these bolts be installed by a carpenter to ensure structural integrity of the deck.

1.1 Item 2(Picture)
GROUND SLOPES TOWARD HOUSE: In some locations the slope of the ground is negative (towards the house). This can cause substantial water intrusion and contributes to water and moisture problems in the home. Water should be directed away from the foundation by correcting the positive slope (away from the house). The correct slope is 1 inch lower per 1 foot away from the house, up to about 4 to 6 feet from the house (for soil) and1/4 inch lower per 1

foot away from the house (for paved surfaces), up to about 4 to 6 feet from the house. Recommend using a soil containing clay in order to deflect water. This work can be done by a landscaper. Please note, in addition to water in the basement, water in the soil near the foundation can create foundation cracking and structural problems due to the freeze/thaw cycle.

Safe Harbor Inspections Inc. Jones
123 School Street
1.3 DRIVEWAY/PARKING AREA
Comments: Maintenance/Repairs
and exterior pressure put on the foundation from soil expanding during a freeze. Water at the foundation also creates an environment ideal for termites and carpenter ants. Therefore, correcting the grading should be considered a high priority.
1.2 Item 1(Picture)
1.2 Item 2(Picture)
Safe Harbor Inspections Inc. Jones
123 School Street
1.4 FLASHINGS
Comments: Maintenance/Repairs
1.5 HANDRAILS/GUARDRAILS
Comments: Maintenance/Repairs
APRON SLOPED INCORRECTLY: The apron at the top of the driveway is sloped in towards the garage. The apron should be sloped away from the garage to prevent water intrusion in the garage. This work can be done by a driveway contractor.
1.3 Item 1(Picture)

FLASHING MISSING: The flashing is missing and should be installed in order to avoid water intrusion behind the siding and possibly into the structure. This work can be done by a siding contractor.
1.4 Item 1(Picture)
Safe Harbor Inspections Inc. Jones
123 School Street
1.6 WINDOWS
Comments: Maintenance/Repairs
2. ROOFING
The inspector shall inspect: the roof covering. The roof drainage systems. The flashings. The skylights, chimneys, and roof penetrations. Describe the roof covering and report the methods used to inspect the roof. The inspector is not required to inspect: Antennae. Interiors of flues or chimneys which are not readily accessible. Other installed accessories.
Styles & Materials
VIEWED ROOF COVERING FROM: WALKED ROOF
TYPE OF ROOF COVERING: ARCHITECTURAL 3-TAB FIBERGLASS
CHIMNEY FLASHING: METAL
CHIMNEY (exterior): BRICK
VENTILATION: SOFFIT VENTS, RIDGE VENTS

HANDRAILS RECOMMENDED: It is recommended that handrails be installed on the steps for safety reasons. This work can be done by a masonry contractor.
1.5 Item 1(Picture)
WINDOW CAULKING: Some of the windows need to be caulked in order to prevent water intrusion. It is recommended that a handyman survey each of the windows and apply the proper caulking as required.
1.6 Item 1(Picture)
Safe Harbor Inspections Inc. Jones
123 School Street
GABLE VENTS, ATTIC FAN

Items

2.0 CHIMNEYS AND ROOF PENETRATIONS

Comments: Maintenance/Repairs

2.1 ROOF COVERING

Comments: Priority. CHIMNEY NEEDS A RAIN COVER: It is recommended that a metal chimney cap be installed on top of the chimney. This will reduce the amount of water and eliminate the possibility of animals coming into the chimney and will also increase the life of the chimney. This work can be done by a chimney contractor.

2.0 Item 1(Picture)

(1) ROOF SHOULD BE REPLACED AS SOON AS POSSIBLE: The roof covering is deteriorated and will need to be replaced as soon as possible. Any weak roof decking and structural members that show deterioration should be replaced at that time. Roof leakage can create wood-rot and damage to the wood roof decking and other framing members, in addition to stains in the ceiling below. Please note, leaking roofs sometimes cause damage that is not visible such as wood rot damage inside walls. Water inside walls is also an attraction for termites and carpenter ants. SIGNS OF PAST OR PRESENT ROOF LEAKS: There are signs of past (or possibly present) roof leaks. My moisture meter did not pick up current moisture content, but it is possible that the stains indicate current roof leakage. It is recommended that this particular area of the roof be monitored for roof leaks. If roof leaks become apparent, a roofing contractor should make the appropriate repairs.

Safe Harbor Inspections Inc. Jones

123 School Street

2.1 Item 1(Picture)

2.1 Item 2(Picture)

Safe Harbor Inspections Inc. Jones

123 School Street

3. KITCHEN

Please see the inspection standards in the "Rooms" section of this report.

4. ROOMS

The inspector shall inspect: the walls, ceilings, and Doors. The steps, stairways, and railings. The countertops and representative number of installed cabinets. A representative number of doors and windows. Garage doors and garage door operators. The inspector is not required to inspect: the paint, wallpaper, and other finish treatments. The carpeting. The window treatments, the central vacuum systems. The household appliances, recreational facilities.

Styles & Materials

TYPE OF WALL MATERIALS:

SHEETROCK

Items

4.0 DOORS (REPRESENTATIVE NUMBER)

Comments: Maintenance/Repairs (2) TWO OR MORE LAYERS OF ROOFING: Two or more layers of roof covering exist. When the roof is replaced, it is recommended that all of the existing roofing materials be removed before the new roofing materials can be installed. Often, the roofing materials do not lay flat. It should also be noted that second and third layers of roofing materials have progressively shorter lives. Please note that some jurisdictions only allow up to 2 layers of roofing. 2.1 Item 3 (Picture)

Safe Harbor Inspections Inc. Jones

123 School Street

4.1 FLOORS

Comments: Maintenance/Repairs

DOOR DOESN'T CLOSE PROPERLY: One or more of the doors does not close properly. Door trimming could help this condition. This can be dealt with by a handyman contractor.
4.0 Item 1(Picture)
(1) BASEMENT FLOOR TILES DETERIORATED: For your information, the basement door
tiles are in a deteriorated condition. These floor tiles can be replaced by a flooring contractor.
4.1 Item 1(Picture)

Safe Harbor Inspections Inc. Jones

123 School Street
4.2 WINDOWS (REPRESENTATIVE NUMBER)
Comments: Maintenance/Repairs
5. BATHROOMS
Please see the inspection standards in the "Rooms" section of this report.

Items
5.0 TOILET
Comments: Maintenance/Repairs (2) FLOOR TILES MAY CONTAIN ASBESTOS: The floor tiles may contain asbestos. These tiles are **not considered a health hazard** unless they are drilled, removed or cut. If desired, removal of these tiles should only
be done by a licensed and qualified asbestos handling contractor.
4.1 Item 2(Picture) SOME ORIGINAL WINDOWS: For your information some of the
windows are original. Consideration for budgeting for replacement in the future is recommended. Also, please note that there may be lead paint involved which should be dealt with by "Lead Paint Safe Practices" and a qualified painting contractor.
4.2 Item 1(Picture)
Safe Harbor Inspections Inc. Jones
123 School Street
6. ATTICS AND CRAWLS
The inspector shall inspect: the insulation and vapor retarders in unfinished spaces. The ventilation of attics and foundation areas. The mechanical ventilation systems. Describe the insulation and vapor retarders in unfinished spaces. The absence of insulation in unfinished spaces at conditioned surfaces. The inspector is not required to: disturb insulation or vapor retarders. Determine indoor air quality.

Styles & Materials
ATTIC INSULATION:
BATT FIBERGLASS
7. STRUCTURAL COMPONENTS

The inspector shall inspect: the structural components, including foundation and framing. By probing a representative number of structural components where deterioration is suspected or where clear indications of possible deterioration exist. Probing is not required when probing would damage the Punished surfaces where no deterioration is visible. Describe the foundation and report the methods used to inspect the underfloor crawl space. The floor structure. The wall structure. The ceiling structure. The roof structure and report the methods used to inspect the attic. The inspector is not required to: provide any engineering service or architectural service. This is an opinion as to the adequacy of any structural system or component.

Styles & Materials

METHOD USED TO OBSERVE CRAWLSPACE: CRAWLED

METHOD USED TO OBSERVE THE ATTIC: CRAWLED A PORTION OF THE ATTIC

CEILING STRUCTURE: WOOD

FOUNDATION: POURED CONCRETE, MASONRY BLOCK

GIRDERS AND BEAMS: WOOD

COLUMNS OR PIERS: STEEL LALLY COLUMNS

FLOOR STRUCTURE: WOOD JOISTS

WALL STRUCTURE: WOOD

ROOF STRUCTURE: WOOD

SIGNS OF WATER INTRUSION: YES

Items

TOILET NOT SECURELY MOUNTED:

The toilet is not mounted securely to the floor. This should be corrected by a licensed plumber

in order to avoid water leakage around the toilet.

5.0 Item 1(Picture)

Safe Harbor Inspections Inc. Jones

123 School Street

7.0 COLUMNS, PIERS AND GIRDERS, BEARING WALLS

Comments: Priority

SUPPORT COLUMNS DO NOT HAVE FOOTINGS: Some of the support columns do not have a solid footing. Correction of this problem should be done in order to ensure proper support for the room above. If you don't fix it right away, monitor for cracks at the base of the column. This work should be done by a general contractor.

STEEL COLUMN NOT FASTENED AT TOP: The steel column is not securely connected to the girder that it is supporting. It is recommended that a secure connection be made by a carpenter in order to insure the stability of the column.

SUPPORT COLUMNS LEANING: Many of the foundation support columns are not vertical. This condition can lead to twisting girders. This can be corrected by a foundation contractor or carpenter.

7.0 Item 1(Picture)

7.0 Item 2(Picture)

Safe Harbor Inspections Inc. Jones

123 School Street

7.1 FLOORS (Structural)

Comments: Maintenance/Repairs

7.2 SIGNS OF WATER INTRUSION

Comments: Maintenance/Repairs FLOOR JOISTS SPLIT: Some of the floor joists are split (horizontally). This condition should be corrected by a carpenter in order to maintain the structural integrity of the floors.

7.1 Item 1(Picture)

VISIBLE SIGNS OF WATER INTRUSION WITH A "MUSTY" SMELL: There are signs of past and/or present moisture. This is indicated by what appears to be discoloration (mold like substance) on some of the walls. A qualified environmental person should be contacted regarding this discoloration and how to deal with it. We are not qualified to state whether this is mold or not and mold is outside the scope of our inspection. Very often, water intrusion into the basement is caused by improper drainage around the perimeter of the house. Proper functioning of the gutters and downspouts is critical. Also, it is critical for the ground to be sloped away from the foundation.

Therefore, it is recommended that a qualified gutter contractor/landscaper evaluate the condition and proper functioning of the drainage systems in order to divert water away from the foundation. If water intrusion is still occurring after correction of surface water problems, recommend contacting a water proofing contractor for further evaluation and pricing alternates. The mold should be dealt with by a qualified mold contractor.

Safe Harbor Inspections Inc. Jones
123 School Street
7.2 Item 1(Picture)
7.2 Item 2(Picture)
7.2 Item 3(Picture)
Safe Harbor Inspections Inc. Jones
123 School Street
7.3 WOOD DESTROYING ORGANISMS (and other pests if noted)
Comments: Priority
7.2 Item 4(Picture)
7.2 Item 5(Picture)
Safe Harbor Inspections Inc. Jones
123 School Street

(1) TERMITE TREATMENT (bait stations): There are termite treatment bait stations at several locations on the exterior perimeter of the home. It should be noted the age and success of the past treatment is not known. Expect hidden damage. Recommend consultation and a termite guarantee with an extermination company.
7.3 Item 1(Picture)
(2) SUBSTANTIAL TERMITE DAMAGE: There is substantial termite damage that will need to be repaired in order to ensure the integrity of the structure. This work should be done by a carpenter or framing contractor. Expect hidden damage and pursue a wood destroying organism guarantee from the seller. Recommend further inspections and treatment by an

exterminator. Note, some work was completed but more is needed.

7.3 Item 2(Picture)

Safe Harbor Inspections Inc. Jones
123 School Street

8. PLUMBING SYSTEM

The inspector shall inspect: the interior water supply and distribution systems including all fixtures and the faucets. The drain, waste, and vent systems including all fixtures. The water heating equipment. The vent systems, flues, and chimneys. The fuel storage and fuel distribution systems. The drainage sumps, sump pumps, and related piping. Describe the water supply, drain, waste, and vent piping materials. The water heating equipment including the energy source. The location of main water and main fuel shut off valves. The inspector is not required to inspect: the clothes washing machine and actions. The interiors of flues or chimneys which are not readily accessible. Wells, well pumps, or water storage related equipment. Water conditioning systems. Solar water heating systems. Fire and law inspect their systems. Private waste disposal systems. Determine: whether water supply and waste disposal systems are public or private. The quantity or quality of water supply. Operate safety valves or shut off valves.

Styles & Materials

PLUMBING SUPPLY PIPING: COPPER
PLUMBING DISTRIBUTION PIPING: COPPER
PLUMBING WASTE AND VENT
PIPES: PVC, CAST IRON
PRESSENCE OF A DRIP LEG FOR
HOT WATER SYSTEM: YES
TYPE OF HOT WATER HEATER: OIL FIRED
APPROXIMATE HOT WATER
HEATER CAPACITY: 50 gallons
WATER SOURCE: PUBLIC
PLUMBING WASTE SYSTEM: PUBLIC (ACCORDING TO SELLER/ SELLERS AGENT)

Items

8.0 DRAIN, WASTE AND VENT SYSTEMS
Comments: Priority
Safe Harbor Inspections Inc. Jones
123 School Street
(1) AMATEUR PLUMBING: There is an amateur plumbing repair which should be corrected by a plumber.
8.0 Item 1(Picture)
(2) PLUMBING WASTE LINE LEAKS: The plumbing waste line leaks and should be repaired by a plumber.
8.0 Item 2(Picture)
Safe Harbor Inspections Inc. Jones
123 School Street

9. ELECTRICAL SYSTEMS

The inspector shall inspect: the service drop. The service entrance conductors, cables, and raceways. The service equipment and main disconnects. The service grounding. The interior components of service panels and sub panels. The conductors. The overcurrent protection devices. A representative number of installed lighting fixtues, switches, and receptacles. The ground fault circuit interrupters. Describe the amperage and voltage rating of the service. The location of main disconnects and sub panels. The wiring methods. Report on the presence of solid conductor aluminum branch circuit wiring. On the absence of smoke detectors. The inspector is not required to inspect: the remote-control devices unless device is the only control device. The alarm systems and components. The low voltage wiring, systems, and components. The ancillary wiring, systems, and components not a part of the primary electrical power distribution system. Measure amperage, voltage, or impedance.

Styles & Materials

PANEL CAPACITY: 100 AMP (must be verified by licensed electrician)
ELECTRICAL SERVICE CONDUCTORS: OVERHEAD SERVICE
MAIN SERVICE VOLTAGE: 240 VOLTS

PANEL TYPE: CIRCUIT BREAKERS
WIRING METHODS: NM (non-metallic)
BRANCH WIRE 15 and 20 AMP: COPPER
SUB-PANEL PRESENT: NO - (AT LEAST NOT VISIBLE)
SMOKE DETECTORS PRESENT: YES - BUT MORE SMOKE DETECTORS RECOMMENDED
CARBON MONOXIDE DETECTORS PRESENT: NONE NOTED - SAFETY ISSUE
Items
9.0 CONNECTED DEVICES AND FIXTURES (Observed from a representative number operation of ceiling fans, lighting fixtures located inside the house, garage, and on the dwelling's exterior walls)
Comments: Priority
(1) LIGHT FIXTURE WIRING EXPOSED: The light fixture is not properly mounted and electrical wires are exposed. This should be corrected by an electrician for safety reasons.
9.0 Item 1(Picture)
Safe Harbor Inspections Inc. Jones
123 School Street
9.1 GFCI (GROUND FAULT CIRCUIT INTERRUPTERS)
Comments: Priority (2) CEILING FAN NOT OPERATING:
At the time of the inspection, the ceiling fan was not operating (this could be a Pre hazard). This unit should be checked/replaced by an electrician for safety reasons.
9.0 Item 2(Picture)
ADDITIONAL (PROPERLY FUNCTIONING) GFCI'S NEEDED: GFCI'S shut themselves off in the event of an electrical fault. For example, if an appliance is plugged in to a GFCI and then falls into a sink filled with water, the GFCI shuts off immediately - you would not get an electrical shock when you went to pick up the appliance. It is highly recommended that properly functioning Ground Fault Circuit Interrupters (GFCI's) be present if they are not already installed in areas such as the kitchen, bathroom, exterior, garage outlets, basements and other areas where there may be water. The installation of GFCI's is considered an important and economical safety

upgrade and can save lives. This work should be done by an electrician. Please note, oftentimes a GFCI is present but is not working correctly. The device should be checked and replaced by an electrician as needed. Some photographs of non-GFCI outlets are included, but not all. Recommend further checking and modifications by an electrician.

Safe Harbor Inspections Inc. Jones
123 School Street
9.2 OUTLETS
Comments: Maintenance/Repairs
9.1 Item 1(Picture)
9.1 Item 2(Picture)
Safe Harbor Inspections Inc. Jones
123 School Street
9.3 PANELS
Comments: Priority (1) COVER PLATE MISSING: At least one cover plate is missing. This is a safety hazard and should be corrected by an electrician or a handyman. All of the switch plates and outlet covers should be inspected and replaced as needed.
9.2 Item 1(Picture)
(2) OUTLET WIRING REVERSED:
The wires are reversed at some of the electrical outlets. This should be corrected by an electrician for safety reasons.
9.2 Item 2(Picture)
Safe Harbor Inspections Inc. Jones
123 School Street
10. HEATING
The home inspector shall observe permanently installed heating systems including: Heating equipment; Normal operating controls; Automatic safety controls; Chimneys, flues, and vents, where readily visible; Solid fuel heating devices; Heat distribution systems including fans, pumps, ducts and piping, with supports, insulation, air filters, registers, radiators, fan coil units, convectors; and the presence of an installed heat source in each room. The home inspector shall describe: Energy

source; and Heating equipment and distribution type. The home inspector shall operate the systems using normal operating controls. The home inspector shall open readily access panels provided by the manufacturer or installer for routine homeowner maintenance. The home inspector is not required to: Operate heating systems when weather conditions or other circumstances may cause equipment damage; Operate automatic safety controls; Ignite or extinguish solid fuel Pres; or Observe: The interior of flues; Fireplace insert flue connections; Humidifiers; Electronic air filters; or The uniformity or adequacy of heat supply to the various rooms.

Styles & Materials

(1) MAIN BREAKER TAMPERED WITH: The main breaker has been bolted to prevent it from tripping. This is an extremely dangerous condition which should be dealt with immediately in order to avoid over-heating the wires and a possible Pre. Replacement of the entire electrical service is recommended.

9.3 Item 1(Picture) (2) RUST/CORROSION ON MAIN PANEL: The main electrical panel is partially rusted and corroded. This is due to water intrusion (water following the main service cables from the outside). This should be further investigated by an electrician for safety reasons.

Whatever recommendations are made by the electrician should be followed.

9.3 Item 2(Picture)

Safe Harbor Inspections Inc. Jones
123 School Street
TYPE OF HEAT SYSTEM: CIRCULATING WATER BOILER
ENERGY SOURCE: OIL
SIGNS OF BURIED OIL TANK: NO
FIRE PROTECTION OVER HEATING UNIT: NO
TYPE OF HEAT DISTRIBUTION SYSTEM: CIRCULATING WATER BASEBOARD
PRESSENSE OF HEAT SOURCE IN EACH ROOM: YES

Items

10.0 FIRE PROTECTION FROM BOILER/FURNACE
Comments: Maintenance/Repairs

10.1 FUEL STORAGE/DISTRIBUTION SYSTEMS
Comments: Priority
10.2 HEAT DISTRIBUTION SYSTEMS (including fans, pumps, ducts and piping, with supports, registers, radiators, fan coil units and convectors)
Comments: Informational
CEILING ABOVE HEATING PLANT NEEDS FIRE PROTECTION: The ceiling above the heating plant should have Pre protection pursuant to normal construction standards. This is fairly simple work and can be accomplished by a heating contractor or carpenter.
10.0 Item 1(Picture) LEAK AT OIL TANK: The oil tank is leaking and should be replaced by an oil tank contractor.
10.1 Item 1(Picture)
Safe Harbor Inspections Inc. Jones
123 School Street
10.3 HEATING EQUIPMENT
Comments: Maintenance/Repairs POSSIBLE ASBESTOS PIPE INSULATION: Some insulation may contain asbestos. Friable asbestos containing material is a health hazard. It is recommended that an asbestos handling contractor be called in to evaluate the insulation. Any recommendations made by this contractor should be followed.
10.2 Item 1(Picture)
HEATING UNIT IS OLD: The heating unit is old but operated at the time of the inspection.
Recommend that you consider replacement of this unit to increase efficiency and on preventive
maintenance basis. This work can be done by a heating contractor.
Safe Harbor Inspections Inc. Jones
123 School Street
10.3 Item 1(Picture)
10.3 Item 2(Picture)
10.3 Item 3(Picture)
Safe Harbor Inspections Inc. Jones
123 School Street

11. AIR CONDITIONING

The home inspector shall observe: Central air conditioning and permanently installed cooling systems including: Cooling and air handling equipment; and Normal operating controls. Distribution systems including: Fans, pumps, ducts and piping, with associated

supports, dampers, insulation, air filters, registers, fan-coil units; and the presence of an installed cooling source in each room. The home inspector shall describe: Energy sources; and Cooling equipment type. The home inspector shall operate the systems using normal operating controls. The home inspector shall open readily access panels provided by the manufacturer or installer for routine homeowner maintenance The home inspector is not required to: Observe window air conditioners or operate cooling systems when weather conditions or other circumstances may cause equipment damage; Observe non-central air conditioners; or Observe the uniformity or adequacy of cool-air supply to the various rooms.

Styles & Materials

COOLING EQUIPMENT TYPE: CENTRAL AIR CONDITIONER UNIT WITH AIR DUCTS AND VENTS

COOLING EQUIPMENT ENERGY SOURCE: ELECTRICITY

12. GENERAL INFORMATION ABOUT THE PROPERTY

Items

12.0 ELECTRICAL MAIN PANEL VIEW

Comments: Informational

12.1 EMERGENCY HEATING SHUT OFF SWITCH LOCATION

Comments: Maintenance/Repairs

12.2 FUEL MAIN SHUT OFF LOCATION

Comments: Informational

12.3 HEATING SYSTEM INFORMATION

Comments: Informational

VIEW OF MAIN ELECTRICAL PANEL IN BASEMENT
12.0 Item 1(Picture) IN STAIRWAY TO THE BASEMENT MAIN FUEL SHUTOFF AT OIL TANK

Safe Harbor Inspections Inc. Jones
123 School Street
HOT WATER HEAT: This heating system utilizes a boiler and a hot water distribution system to keep the house warm. The DVANTAGES of this system include: 1) It provides even and consistent heat in comparison to forced hot air heat. 2) It does not create drafts in rooms as does forced hot air heat. 3) It is usually quieter than forced hot air heating systems. 4) It will not circulate odors through the home like forced hot air heating systems. 5) Hot water heating systems do not have air ducts which take up more space in closets and ceilings. 6) Hot water heating systems do not dry out the air as do force hot air systems (unless humidification systems have been added). 7) Hot water boilers do not have the potential to immediately distribute carbon monoxide throughout the house as does a forced hot air system. If a heat exchanger malfunctions, in a forced hot air system, carbon monoxide can be distributed throughout the house via the duct work and fan system. Therefore, carbon monoxide detectors throughout the house (installed pursuant to manufacturers recommendations) are highly recommended with forced hot air heating systems. The DISADVANTAGES of the system include: 1) Central air conditioning must be a totally separate system (air conditioning systems cannot be "piggybacked" onto hot water heating systems). 2) There is a wider
12.3 Item 1(Picture)
Safe Harbor Inspections Inc. Jones
123 School Street
12.4 WATER MAIN VALVE LOCATION
Comments: Informational
13. GENERAL RECOMMENDATIONS
Items
13.0 AIR DUCT CLEANING
Comments: Informational
13.1 BACK FLOW PREVENTER
Comments: Informational
13.2 GET WARRANTIES FROM SELLERS

Comments: Informational variety of hot air furnaces on the market in comparison to hot water heating boilers. 3) Hot water boilers are more expensive than hot air systems. 4) Hot water radiators take up more space in rooms than hot air registers. 5) Hot water boilers produce pressurized water which can be dangerous in the event of a system malfunction.
MAIN WATER VALVE LOCATED IN BASEMENT
12.4 Item 1(Picture)
AIR DUCT CLEANING: It is recommended that you consult with a professional duct cleaner regarding cleaning the components of the HEATING AND A/C system. Dust can build up and cause mold, indoor air quality issues and lower the efficiency of the A/C system.
BACKFLOW PREVENTER: For your information, a backflow device is designed to prevent water from coming from the landscaping irrigation system back into the house and the public water system. The backflow preventer should be tested on an annual basis. They can fail in a number of ways including leaking and flooding the basement (if it's interior). Contact a plumber that is certified in testing backflow prevention devices. This is for your personal protection.
Always secure copies of warranties for work done on the building, including appliances, heating and cooling systems, roofing and siding, waterproofing systems etc. These written warranties may prove to be very important in the future. A real property inspection is not at all a warrantee. In fact, no warrantee is covered or should be expected. Your inspection should not be considered.

Safe Harbor Inspections Inc. Jones
123 School Street 13.3 HEATING/AIR CONDITIONING SERVICE CONTRACT
Comments: Informational
13.4 KEEP GUTTERS CLEAN
Comments: Informational
13.5 SEAL ATTIC ACCESS
Comments: Informational

13.6 SMOKE AND CARBON MONOXIDE DETECTORS
Comments: Informational
13.7 TERMITES AND OTHER PESTS
Comments: Informational to be a complete list of defects. Remember, only visual items were inspected. An inspector cannot see inside pipes, walls, appliances and equipment. Therefore, expect to discover issues that we're not apparent at the inspection - this will more than likely occur.

AIR-CONDITIONING/HEATING SYSTEM SERVICE CONTRACT RECOMMENDED:
It is recommended that you enter into a service contract with an air-conditioning/heating system contractor for preventive maintenance on the air-conditioning and heating system and have the contract take effect before the closing. Also, have the service contractor accompany you at the final walkthrough and check the heating and A/C system (if one is present) for proper operation before the closing.

KEEP GUTTERS CLEAN: Cleaning the gutters should be done as needed, often 2 or 3 times per year. If the gutters don't drain properly it can result in basement water. Therefore, they should be checked often.

SEAL AIR PATHWAYS FROM THE HOUSE TO THE ATTIC: Mold can grow on surfaces in the attic if warm moist air from the interior of the home comes in contact with cooler surfaces and condenses into water. Therefore, it is very important to seal any pathways against air movement from inside the home and into the attic. This includes replacing old recessed lighting fixtures because they enable air movement. Also make sure the attic hatch and/or the attic stairs are

sealed and insulated to prevent airflow. Sealing against air movement will also substantially reduce energy usage as well because it will reduce the outgrow of warm air in the winter and cool air in the summer. If you obtain a home energy audit, air leakage will be clearly determined, and corrections can be made. Therefore, it is recommended that you contact an energy audit firm and follow their recommendations for health and safety reasons as well as to save energy and money.

ADDITIONAL SMOKE AND CARBON MONOXIDE DETECTORS RECOMMENDED: It is recommended that additional smoke and carbon monoxide detectors get installed by a licensed and qualified electrician pursuant to the applicable building codes of the municipality for personal safety reasons.

Safe Harbor Inspections Inc. Jones
123 School Street
14. HOME WARRANTY INFORMATION
Items
14.0 THIS HOME IS ELIGIBLE FOR A RENEWABLE ONE-YEAR HOME WARRANTY
Comments:
ANNUAL PEST AND TERMITE INSPECTIONS HIGHLY RECOMMENDED: Vermin, subterranean termites and other pests are part of the natural habitat, but they often invade homes. Rodents have collapsible rib cages and can squeeze through even the tiniest crevices. And it is not uncommon for them to establish colonies within crawlspaces, attics, closets, and even the space inside walls, where they can breed and become a health-hazard. Subterranean Termites can enter the home through a tiny crack in the foundation and cause damage to wood framing members **without being able to be visually detected**. Therefore, it would be prudent to have an exterminator evaluate the residence initially (prior to purchasing the home, and regularly thereafter in order to take the appropriate action necessary to eliminate or reduce the potential for intrusion of wood destroying insects and other pests. **It is also recommended that you purchase a Wood Destroying Insect Guarantee from a licensed extermination company.** This will involve an initial Wood Destroying Insect inspection by the extermination company and entering into a service contract and guarantee program. The guarantee involves annual inspections; if wood destroying insects are discovered, the extermination company provides the treatment at their cost. It is also recommended that you seriously consider the idea of having a "preventive maintenance" termite treatment bait station system installed by your exterminator. These

systems are long term management programs requiring annual contracts and utilize termite baits and poisons that are intended to irradiate subterranean termite nests in the vicinity of homes. **Remember that termites and carpenter ants can be present in a home and not be visible and not be detected by an inspector.**

HOME WARRANTY AVAILABLE: This home inspection can be supplemented with a one-year renewable home warranty. The warranty is covered by HomeGauge (a national home inspection

software provider) in conjunction with Global Home USA. Safe Harbor Inspections Inc. receives no compensation associated with this warranty and is not associated, owned by or controlled by either of these companies. As you would expect, the policy covers items that fail or become defective after the home inspection. But the warrantee program is unique in that it also provides coverage even for items that were defective but were unable to be detected or were missed by the Home Inspector at the time of the inspection. The warranty can be purchased for up to 90 days after the home inspection takes place. It can be paid for at the closing table and sometimes can even be included in the mortgage loan. Items included in the one year home warranty if purchased are: Furnaces, Boilers, Heat Pumps, Central Air Conditioners, Electrical System, Thermostats, Water heater System, Plumbing, Polybutylene lines, Sump Pump, Whirlpools, Dishwasher, Food Waste Disposer, Cooking Range/Oven, Microwave, Kitchen Refrigerator, Trash Compactor, Plumbing Fixtures and Faucets.

Safe Harbor Inspections Inc. Jones
123 School Street
Domestic Water Softener, Clearing of Line Stoppage, Well Water System, Refrigerant Recapture and Disposal, Permits in conjunction with a covered repair, Code Violations in conjunction with a covered repair, Improper installation or modification, Removal of defective equipment, Fireplace gas burner, Attic and Exhaust fans, Humidifiers, Dehumidifiers,

Electronic Air Filtering Devices, Door bell System, Lighting Fixtures, Septic Lines, Ejector pump. For more information and to compare warranties or purchase this warranty, please click on the Warranty cover beside your uploaded report at the Home Gauge website (this is where you view your report on-line). The warranty program is highly recommended by Safe Harbor Inspections because it gives you a level of protection that cannot, and will not be covered by Safe Harbor (because the inspection by itself is not a warrantee pursuant to the pre-inspection agreement that you signed and agreed to). This warrantee program is specifically designed for clients that have received a home inspection and ultimately purchased the home. If you elect not to purchase this warranty, do not expect Safe Harbor Inspections Inc. to act like a warranty company. Again, your inspection should not be construed as a warranty.

HOME WARRANTY AVAILABLE: This home inspection can be supplemented with a one-year renewable home warranty. The warranty is covered by Home Gauge (a national home inspection software provider) in conjunction with Global Home USA. Safe Harbor Inspections Inc. receives no compensation associated with this warranty and is not associated, owned by or controlled by either of these companies. As you would expect, the policy covers items that fail or become defective after the home inspection. But the warrantee program is unique in that it also provides coverage even for items that were defective but were unable to be detected or were missed by the Home Inspector at the time of the inspection. The warranty can be purchased for up to 90 days after the home inspection takes place. It can be paid for at the closing table and sometimes can even be included in the mortgage loan. Items included in the one year home warranty if purchased are: Furnaces, Boilers, Heat Pumps, Central Air Conditioners, Electrical System, Thermostats, Water heater System, Plumbing, Polybutylene lines, Sump Pump, Whirlpools, Dishwasher, Food Waste Disposer, Cooking Range/Oven, Microwave, Kitchen Refrigerator, Trash Compactor, Plumbing Fixtures and Faucets,

Domestic Water Softener, Clearing of Line Stoppage, Well Water System, Refrigerant Recapture and Disposal, Permits in conjunction with a covered repair, Code Violations in conjunction with a covered repair, Improper installation or modification, Removal of defective equipment, Fireplace gas burner, Attic and Exhaust fans, Humidifiers, Dehumidifiers, Electronic Air Filtering Devices, Door bell System, Lighting Fixtures, Septic Lines, Ejector pump. For more information and to compare warranties or purchase this warranty, please click on the Warranty cover beside your uploaded report at the Home Gauge website (this is where you view your report on-line). The warranty program is highly recommended by Safe Harbor Inspections because it gives you a level of protection that cannot, and will not be covered by Safe Harbor (because the inspection by itself is not a warrantee pursuant to the pre-inspection agreement that you signed and agreed to). This warrantee program is specifically designed for clients that have received a home inspection and ultimately purchased the home. If you elect not to purchase this warranty, do not expect Safe Harbor Inspections Inc. to act like a warranty company. Again, your inspection should not be construed as a warranty.

Safe Harbor Inspections Inc. Jones
123 School Street
15. ITEMS/COMPONENTS NOT INSPECTED
Often during Home Inspections there are conditions which exist that prevent a full inspection of certain components of the home. Following is a description of some of those conditions occurring during this inspection. It is recommended that you follow up
with additional inspections or investigation of these items as soon as possible and before the real estate closing.
Items
15.0 AIR-CONDITIONING SYSTEM
Comments: Informational
15.1 FINISHED BASEMENT

Comments: Not Inspected
15.2 BEHIND WALLS AND CEILINGS
Comments: Not Inspected
15.3 BELOW CARPETS AND FURNITURE
Comments: Not Inspected
TOO COLD TO OPERATE AIR-CONDITIONING COMPRESSOR: According to manufacturers
specifications when the outside temperature is below 65° the compressor should not be turned on because it could cause damage to the unit. At the time of the inspection the temperature was below 65°, therefore, it's operation could not be tested. However, the fan can be turned on regardless of outside temperature so its operation was checked. FINISHED BASEMENT PREVENTS FULL INSPECTION: Portions of the basement floors, walls and ceiling are covered by finishing materials. Therefore, most of the plumbing, electrical, and structural systems, including the location for where termites are typically discovered were not visible at the time of the inspection. It is possible that there are hidden defects that were not discovered during this inspection as a result of the finished basement, including termites. (Please note that the scope of home and termite inspections only includes inspection of visible and accessible components.)

CAN'T SEE BEHIND WALLS AND CEILINGS: The inspector can't see behind walls and ceilings and as a result, there may be defects that were not detected during the inspection. Examples of this are 1) termite damage, 2) water leaks, wood rot, electrical wiring issues. When walls and ceilings get removed, sometimes these things become apparent.
Safe Harbor Inspections Inc. Jones
123 School Street
15.4 CERTIFICATES OF OCCUPANCY/PROPERTY BOUNDRIES
Comments: Not Inspected
15.5 LAWN IRRIGATION SYSTEM
Comments: Not Inspected

15.6 NO SEARCH OF PUBLIC RECORDS

Comments: Not Inspected

CAN'T SEE BELOW CARPETS AND FURNITURE/STORAGE: Be aware that there is no visibility below carpets, storage items (boxes etc) and furniture. Therefore, when you move in and the house is empty, defects may be visible that were not visible at the time of the inspection. NO SEARCH FOR CERTIFICATES OF OCCUPANCY/PROPERTY BOUNDARIES NOT CHECKED: Most modifications to homes such as decks, finished basements, additions, dormers etc. require the owner to obtain permits and final municipal approvals (certificates of occupancy (C of O's). The process includes inspections during construction or modification. (Even replacement decks require demolition permits and new deck permits.) In homes that do not have the appropriate C of O's, obtaining them requires inspections (which may require physical modifications) and ultimately may impact the real estate taxes on the home.

The home inspection DOES NOT INCLUDE A SEARCH FOR PROPER CERTIFICATES OF OCCUPANCY. It is recommended that you discuss this situation with your attorney and make sure you understand the status of C of O's, municipal inspections and permits. Property boundaries not established. The home inspection does not include a property survey which establishes boundaries by special instruments and procedures. Location of fences and structures relative to property boundaries and zoning is not a part of a home inspection.

LAWN IRRIGATION SYSTEM NOT OPERATED: The lawn irrigation system was not operated because the system had been winterized. NO SEARCH OF PUBLIC RECORDS: This home inspection does not include any search of public records whatsoever. Therefore, there may be defects in the real estate that were not discovered during the home inspection. For example, fences may not be on the property line; there may have been past floods or Pres impacting the home; there may be title defects, or issues pending at the building department. It is our recommendation that you discuss all of these items with your attorney for your protection.

Safe Harbor Inspections Inc. Jones
123 School Street
16. HOME INSPECTION EXPECTATIONS
Safe Harbor Inspections Inc. Jones
123 School Street
WHAT IS A HOME INSPECTION: An incredibly diverse, multi-disciplined consulting service, delivered under difficult in-field circumstances, before a highly stressed, sometimes hostile audience with direct buyer and seller interests, in an impossibly short time frame, requiring the production of an extraordinarily detailed technical report, almost instantly, without benefit of research facilities or resources.
WARNING: This inspection is a best effort only, and due to time, complexity and a multitude of other limitations with the inspection, we will definitely not identify all the defects in the building. Do not rely on this inspection and report for your negotiations with the seller.

Suggested expectations for your home inspection:
Your expectations regarding a home inspection should be reasonable and realistic. Therefore, following are some basic points that are standard within the home inspection industry throughout the United States. Please keep these points in mind as time goes on after the inspection.
• **Inspectors can only inspect what is visible.** For example, inspectors cannot see inside of pipes, walls, equipment, machinery, above ceiling tiles, behind insulation or storage materials, etc. Sometimes, termites are active inside of the wall without any outward appearance of their presence until someone starts construction, removes the wall and then they become visible. In addition, sometimes, there is no access to certain parts of the home, or certain components or systems of the home. Perhaps the garage was filled with boxes, access to

the crawl space was blocked, or there was a freezer in front of the main electrical panel. It was impossible observe the conditions of these components during the inspection. Please don't blame the inspector for things that were not visible during the inspection.

• **Inspectors observe and report on conditions effective on the date of the inspection.** Because building systems and components are in a constant state of "wearing out" and things change as time goes on, inspectors can only observe conditions as of the date of the

inspection, not a week, a month or a year later. As an example, during the inspection there were no cracks in the foundation, however, after some slight settlement a crack developed. Hopefully

you understand that you should expect that components might be ready to fail without any outward or visible signs, and things change over time.

• **Inspectors check to see if a component is doing its major function, not minor functions.** For example, a heating operates and puts out heat during the inspection, but one of the radiators does not function correctly, or perhaps the thermostat operates, but not well. These small items may or may not be discovered during the inspection. It is reasonable for you to expect that certain malfunctions were not detected during the inspection.

• **This is not a code compliance inspection or certi1cation.** It is almost impossible for an inspector to accurately state whether an item is within code or not. For example, a house built in 1920 may have been built without any code in effect, therefore, it is "grandfathered". Grandfathering means code modifications after the date of the construction are not applicable. In addition, different municipalities adopt different state and federal codes at different times. Another complicating factor is attributable to the complexity of codes: for example, there may be 10 different code measurements/requirements applicable to a staircase. The only way to see if something is "within code" is to have it checked by the municipal code inspector. Even the municipal code inspector may not take into consideration certain elements of the code.

• **Home inspections do not imply any kind of warranty or guarantee of the structure or components**. For all of the reasons described above, Home inspectors do not guarantee the condition of homes.

• **If you think the inspector made an error, contact the inspector and discuss the situation.** The inspector will likely want to visit the home and see and understand the situation directly. Usually, things can be explained and put into proper perspective.

• **It's easy to "Monday morning quarterback."** Sometimes, a contractor is called in to make repairs or review certain conditions. Often, these contractors will say "your inspector should have seen this - he must've been blind!' Keep in mind, that your inspector observed conditions as of a particular date, and looked at hundreds of components in the building in a short timeframe from a generalist's perspective. It is guaranteed that certain things will not be detected or reported on during the inspection for the reasons explained above. So, watch out for Monday morning quarterbacking by a contractor.

• . ALWAYS USE LICENSED CONTRACTORS - IF YOU DON'T, EXPECT POOR QUALITY WORK. ONLY LICENSED CONTRACTORS SHOULD BE INVITED ONTO YOU PROPERTY
FOR QUALITY OF WORK AND LIABILITY REASONS.
ALWAYS ASK FOR PROOF THAT THEY ARE LICENSED.
17. New York State Standards of Practice and
Code of Ethics
Items
17.0 NEW YORK STATE CODE OF ETHICS AND STANDARDS OF PRACTICE FOR HOME INSPECTORS
Comments: Informational
18. FINAL WALK THROUGH CHECK LIST
Items

18.0 CHECK LIST
Comments: Informational

CLOSING/WALK-THROUGH CHECKLIST

BASEMENT:
____ Look at the walls for any signs of leaks.
____ Make sure all stored items are removed.
COOLING AND HEATING SYSTEMS:
____ Turn the thermostat to a higher setting. Feel each radiator or register for warmth.
____ In the summer months, (exterior air temperature must be higher than 60 degrees) turn the air conditioning to a lower setting. Feel each register or room unit for cool air.
____ Obtain copies of all manufacturers manuals and warranties for the heating system and air conditioning system if available.
____ Obtain the name of the heating or air conditioning contractor presently servicing the system.
____ If the heating system is a heat pump or electric baseboard system, you should obtain copies of the last 12 months electric bills to estimate your energy cost.
____ Operate all ceiling fans.
PLUMBING AND BATHROOMS:
____ Run the water in all the sinks at the same time and flush the toilet to check the pressure.
____ Turn on the hot and cold water in each fixture.
____ If there is a landscape sprinkler system turn it on and operate all zones to confirm proper operation.
____ Turn on all hose bibs.
____ Operate all fans.
ELECTRICAL:
____ Turn all light fixtures on and off.
____ Test all smoke detectors.
____ If any work has been performed on the electrical system since the home inspection, obtain The Fire Underwriters Certificate for same.

____ Test all alarm systems. Obtain copies of all warranties and operating manuals. Get information concerning any central monitoring companies as well as a copy of their security agreement. Change all security codes immediately after closing.

KITCHENS AND APPLIANCES:

____ Turn on the faucet and sprayer.

____ Operate all appliances, fans and range hoods. Don't forget the washer and dryer, run through all their cycles.

____ Check the brands of all appliances to make sure they have not been replaced.

WINDOWS AND DOORS:

____ Open and close all windows and operate all locks.

____ Open and close all doors and operate all locks.

____ Operate any automatic garage door openers and obtain the transmitters.

____ Operate all door bells and intercoms.

____ Change all exterior locks immediately after closing.

ROOFS, GUTTERS AND DOWNSPOUTS:

____ Check the interior of the home for leaks.

____ Look for missing shingles, shakes, or tiles.

____ Check to see that gutters and downspouts are secure.

FIREPLACES AND STOVES:

____ Make sure your attorney has a c/o for the stove or fireplace.

____ Obtain operating and installation instructions for stoves if available.

Safe Harbor Inspections Inc. Jones
123 School Street

INVOICE
Safe Harbor Inspections Inc.
PO Box 623
Huntington, New York
11743
631-275-8080
Inspected By: James H. Ruppert

Inspection Date: 10/29/2018
Report ID: 123 School Street
Customer Info: Inspection Property:
Mr. and Mrs. Jones 123 School Street
Any Town NY 11777

Inspection Fee:
Service Price Amount Sub-Total
Tax $0.00
Total Price $0.00
Payment Method:
Payment Status:
Note:
Safe Harbor Inspections Inc. Jones
123 School Street
This report was prepared by:
Safe Harbor Inspections Inc.
James H. Ruppert
NYS Home Inspector License NY 16000008389
Department of Environmental Conservation (Termite)
License C183970
PO Box 623
Huntington, NY 11743
631-275-8080

Thank you for the opportunity to be of service to you.
Safe Harbor Inspections Inc. Jones
123 School Street Inspector SAFE HARBOR INSPECTIONS
INC.
Pre-Inspection Agreement
THIS AGREEMENT CONTAINS A LIMITATION OF LIABILITY
ON THE PART OF THE HOME INSPECTION COMPANY AND
THE HOME INSPECTOR. PLEASE READ IT CAREFULLY.
THIS IS INTENDED TO BE A LEGALLY BINDING
AGREEMENT. IF YOU DO NOT FULLY UNDERSTAND IT,
SEEK THE ADVICE OF AN
ATTORNEY BEFORE SIGNING.

Name: Mr. and Mrs. Jones, Address of home to be inspected: 123 School Street, Any Town, NY 11777 Inspector's Name: James H. Ruppert Inspector's NYS License #: NY 16000008389 Safe Harbor Inspections Inc., (including its employees, subcontractors, agents, and inspectors), hereinafter referred to as "COMPANY" will perform a onetime visual inspection in accordance with the HOME INSPECTION LAWS OF THE STATE OF NEW YORK, I.E the STANDARDS OF PRACTICE and CODE OF ETHICS copies of which are available on the NYS Department of State website www.dos.state.ny.us . Home inspectors are licensed by the NYS Department of State. Home Inspectors may only report on readily accessible and observed conditions as outlined in this pre-inspection agreement, Article 12 B of the Real Property Law and the regulations promulgated there under including, but not limited to, the Code of Ethics and Regulations and the Standards of Practice as provided in Title 19 NYCRR Subparts 197-4 and 197-5 et seq. Home inspectors are not permitted to provide engineering or architectural services. Prior hereto, there has been no agreement between the parties other than that a COMPANY Inspector would meet CUSTOMER at the premises to possibly enter into this agreement. All prior agreements, both real and imagined, both oral and written, are merged into this pre-inspection agreement and it alone sets forth all the terms and conditions of the agreement between the parties. No CUSTOMER changes are valid unless approved in a separate writing, signed by an officer of the COMPANY. If the Report is sent to CUSTOMER over the internet, COMPANY assumes no liability if CUSTOMER is unable to download or view the electronic version of the Report.

THE WRITTEN REPORT WILL INCLUDE THE FOLLOWING ONLY: structural condition, electrical system, plumbing, water heater, heating system, air conditioning system, condition of major systems, general interior including ceilings, walls, floors, windows, insulation, and attic ventilation; general exterior including roof, gutter system, chimney, drainage, grading and an inspection for WDI (wood destroying insects is included). It is understood and agreed that this inspection will only be of readily accessible areas of the dwelling and is limited to visual observations of apparent conditions existing at the time of the inspection. CUSTOMER acknowledges that the Report is not to be considered a substitute for a seller's Property Condition Disclosure Statement.

THE INSPECTOR IS NOT REQUIRED TO: move furniture, personal goods or equipment that may impede access or limit visibility. The Inspector is not required to evaluate or inspect the following: intercoms, security systems, fences, timers, backflow preventers, water conditioning equipment, cosmetic items, swimming pools, hot tubs, whirlpools, Jacuzzis (and ancillary components), wells, cesspools/sewer pipes, the presence/absence of rodents or insects, security, telephone, wiring circuit logic and switch locations, music and computer systems, central vacuum systems, water softeners, radiant heat systems, internal component heat exchangers, thermostatic or time-clock controls, Pre and smoke detectors, sprinkler systems, sheds, or other "out-buildings", Pre and safety equipment. Design problems and adequacies are not within the scope of the inspection. The Inspector will not determine the operational capacity, quality or suitability for a particular use of the items inspected. The inspection does not determine compliance or noncompliance with manufacturer's specifications; past or present. Soil conditions, geological stability, engineering analysis are beyond the scope and purpose of this inspection and are not included in this report. This is not a compliance inspection or certification for past or present governmental codes, rules or regulations of any kind. NO search or check of municipal records or property boundaries (land survey) is included. Latent, hidden and concealed defects and deficiencies are excluded from the inspection and report. The inspection and report do not address and are not intended to address the presence or danger from any potentially harmful substances and environmental hazards including but not limited to radon gas, carbon monoxide, lead, lead paint, asbestos, Chinese drywall, sound proofing, buried or above ground fuel storage tanks, urea formaldehyde, various molds and spores, water quality, toxic or flammable chemicals or gases and water and airborne hazards. The inspector is not required to climb on the roof, enter crawl spaces or attics where the ceiling height is less than 4 feet, lacks flooring, or otherwise inaccessible, and does not perform invasive procedures: equipment, items and systems will not be dismantled. Areas above ceilings are inaccessible, including dropped ceilings. The inspector only uses normal operating devices and performs no destructive or disruptive testing procedures.

NOT A WARRANTY The parties agree that COMPANY and its employees and agents, assume no liability or responsibility for the cost of repairing or replacing any reported or unreported defects of deficiencies, either current or arising in the future, or for any property damage, consequential damage, or bodily injury of any nature. THE INSPECTION AND REPORT ARE NOT INTENDED TO BE A GUARANTEE OR WARRANTY, EXPRESS OR IMPLIED, REGARDING THE ADEQUACY, PERFORMANCE, OR CONDITION OF ANY INSPECTED STRUCTURE, ITEM, OR SYSTEM.COMPANY IS NOT AN INSURER OF ANY INSPECTED CONDITIONS.

DISPUTES: It is specifically agreed that no lawsuit or other type of claim of any kind arising out of or in any way relating to this AGREEMENT, the inspection or the Report shall be made unless each of the following conditions is satisfied first, in order: Written notice of the claim must be given to the COMPANY on or before the 10th day after the date of discovery of a claimed defect or the date said claimed defect should have been discovered. The notice shall: (a) describe the claim including what the CUSTOMER believes COMPANY did or failed to do; (b) state why CUSTOMER believes the COMPANY is responsible; (c) state what CUSTOMER believes COMPANY should do about it and; (d) order to allow COMPANY to re-inspect as required in the following paragraph. Notice shall be sent by Certified mail, RRR to the COMPANY at **PO Box 623, Huntington, NY 11743**

RIGHT TO RE-INSPECT: If CUSTOMER believes the COMPANY made a mistake, before making any repairs or alterations relating to the alleged mistake, CUSTOMER shall notify COMPANY and provide COMPANY a reasonable opportunity to inspect the portion of the property relating to the alleged mistake. Failure to so notify the Company and allow an inspection shall bar any claims being made.

Any dispute, controversy, interpretation or claim including claims for, but not limited to, breach of contract, any form of negligence, fraud, or misinterpretation arising out of, from or related to, this contract or arising out of, from or related to the inspection or inspection report shall be submitted first to a Non-Binding Mediation conference and absent a voluntary settlement through Non-Binding Mediation to be followed by final and Binding Arbitration, if necessary, as conducted by Construction Dispute Resolution Services, LLC or Resolute Systems, Inc. utilizing their respective Rules and Procedures. If you would like to utilize the Mediation or Arbitration services of another dispute resolution provider other than one of those so stated please submit your recommendation us for our consideration. If the dispute is submitted to Binding Arbitration, the decision of the Arbitrator appointed there under shall be final and binding and the enforcement of the Arbitration Award may be entered in any Court or administrative tribunal having jurisdiction thereof. NOTICE: YOU AND WE WOULD HAVE A RIGHT OR OPPORTUNITY TO LITIGATE DISPUTES THROUGH A COURT AND HAVE A JUDGE OR JURY DECIDE THE DISPUTES BUT HAVE AGREED INSTEAD TO RESOLVE DISPUTES THROUGH MEDIATION AND BINDING ARBITRATION.

Any arbitration claim, lawsuit, or other type of claim must be Pled within ONE YEAR OF THE DATE OF THIS AGREEMENT.

Venue of any arbitration claim brought by either party must be brought in the County of Nassau, State of New York and any lawsuit brought by either party must be brought in the Supreme Court or local District Courts of the County of Nassau, State of New York, without a jury, including counterclaims and third-party claims. CUSTOMER agrees that if COMPANY is ever subpoenaed or summoned to appear in a court action or arbitration matter (hereinafter "Hearing") by CUSTOMER or anyone else because of the COMPANY'S inspection of the building identified above and/or any of its components or other portions of the premises where it is located, that CUSTOMER will either reimburse COMPANY for attending said Hearing at the rate of $200.00 per hour, including travel time, or obtain a court order quashing said subpoena or dismissing said summons, all at CUSTOMER'S sole cost and expense."

LIMITATION OF INSPECTORS LIABILITY: The purpose of this provision is to limit the amount of money damages that CUSTOMER may claim and recover from COMPANY. The maximum amount of money that CUSTOMER may claim and recover is hereby limited to the fee paid by CUSTOMER to the COMPANY under this Agreement.

This limitation applies to every type of claim or cause of action arising out of or in any way related to this agreement, the inspection or report, including but not limited to claims for damages, costs, expenses, demands, controversies, actions, debts, compensation, or causes of action of whatever nature or character, whether based on a tort, contract, extra contractual duty, malfeasance, misfeasance or other theory of recovery, including, but not limited to, claims for breach of contract (actual or implied), negligence, malfeasance, misfeasance and any and all other extra contractual duties, for all actual damages, all exemplary and punitive damages, and property damage which the Customer may have concerning any such breach of contract, negligence, or negligent misrepresentation claims alleged to have occurred by the action or inaction of the COMPANY or any of its employees or Inspector. This limitation does not apply to any claim for vexatious litigation or similar type of claim by COMPANY against CUSTOMER or CUSTOMER'S lawyer. CUSTOMER agrees to pay COMPANY'S reasonable legal fees in any action where the COMPANY substantially prevails in any court of law and/or where this agreement and its limitation of liability clause is held to be valid.

CUSTOMERS Initials __________.

CUSTOMER agrees that this agreement may be executed by facsimile which shall constitute an original. It is also understood and agreed that an acceptance of the terms and conditions contained herein by the CUSTOMER shall be just as binding if made electronically by computer or over the internet. The person who signs this agreement represents that they have the full authority to sign on behalf of all named CUSTOMERS. If any named CUSTOMER denies the authority to sign, the person signing agrees to hold the Company harmless for all costs, expenses and damages, including judgments that may be entered against COMPANY and its reasonable legal fees, if COMPANY incurs same as a result of said denial of authority. In the event any provision of this agreement is determined to be invalid or unenforceable, the other provisions shall remain valid and enforceable and in full force and in effect. The report is intended for the use of the above-named customer only and no other person or entity may rely on the report for any reason. If immediate threats to health or safety are observed during the course of the inspection, the client hereby consents to allow the home inspector to disclose such immediate threats to health or safety to the property owner and/or occupants of the property. It is agreed that buyer's agent will receive a copy of the inspection report. CUSTOMER agrees to hold harmless and indemnify COMPANY for losses, fees and costs incurred as a result of any third-party action that may include COMPANY relative to the report.

Furthermore, any third party reviewing this report for any reason shall be bound by the terms and conditions of this Inspection Agreement which is an integral part of the report. CUSTOMER understands and agrees that by law he/she must sign this Agreement and this agreement will form a part of the inspection report and acceptance of the inspection report by CUSTOMER and payment thereof will constitute acceptance of the terms and conditions of this agreement. If CUSTOMER does not agree to the terms hereof, CUSTOMER may obtain a full refund of the fee if written notice is sent to the COMPANY prior to the inspection Report being sent out and if CUSTOMER executes a general release in favor of the COMPANY and its officers, employees and shareholders. TECHNICALLY EXHAUSTIVE INSPECTION AVAILABLE: CUSTOMER is advised that there is a technically exhaustive inspection available with a lower liability limit of the visual inspection, and that a fee for this type of inspection could be $5,000.00 or more, depending on the home. The Company will need to retain other specialists as necessary to prepare a technically exhaustive report. A request in writing for this service must be accompanied by a 50% deposit required to commence this inspection.

AGREED TO BY CUSTOMER
Mr. and Mrs. Jones, 10/29/2018
AGREED TO BY COMPANY:
James H. Ruppert, President, 10/29/2018
Safe Harbor Inspections Inc. Jones

Client testimonials

Thank you to Kevin and his team from the bottom of our hearts! We knew right away when Kevin welcomed us into his office, he was the one and we were right!!!! The same team from beginning to end and we didn't want to say "goodbye" to everyone when we were done. We felt like they were family and we love everything about our new home. We got so many compliments from friends and family. We highly recommend him and his team. I wish I could give more than 5 stars. We'll give them 100 stars :). S.Y.

*

Just a great experience with Kevin! Great advice and suggestions when I needed them most. Kevin is a man of his word which is difficult to find these days. I am proud to give him the highest recommendation to anyone. M.T.

*

We are so happy to have proceeded with Kevin Sime. Kevin could not have been more accommodating managed to solve any issue that arose throughout the process and made our dream come true within a timely manner. Kevin had a great understanding of what we wanted to achieve, along with timing and execution. He went above and beyond and we could not be more thankful. We can only highly recommend him! S.D.

I really would like to thank you for trying and actually would like to commend you on your professionalism and enthusiasm in helping us in our search! This is something that's unfortunately not so common in real estate agents these days. N.S.

*

Kevin is the go to guy for everything in Long Beach and the surrounding area. He knows the market, what different neighborhoods are like in and off season ("at 2 in the morning that place is a zoo" actual quote). He also knows the restoration business, so if that place you like needs a new kitchen, you can get a good sense of what will be involved working with Kevin. You can't go wrong using Kevin on any deal. D.D.

*

Kevin is a true professional and a great partner to work with. He worked with our time schedule and he also made a lot of good suggestions that helped guide our decisions. I would highly recommend him and we will certainly use him again in the future. J.M

*

I found Kevin Sime to be extremely reliable and to be true to his word and trustworthy. This is the second time that I have used his services and I will do so again, when and if the need arises. He is dependable and has a very capable staff that does thorough work. I have recommend Kevin to friends and family and will continue to do so. D.C

9 781694 950666